Cambridge Elements

Elements in the Psychology of Religion
edited by
Jonathan Lewis-Jong
St Mary's University Twickenham and University of Oxford

DIVINATION

A Cognitive Perspective

Ze Hong
University of Macau

CAMBRIDGE
UNIVERSITY PRESS

Shaftesbury Road, Cambridge CB2 8EA, United Kingdom

One Liberty Plaza, 20th Floor, New York, NY 10006, USA

477 Williamstown Road, Port Melbourne, VIC 3207, Australia

314–321, 3rd Floor, Plot 3, Splendor Forum, Jasola District Centre,
New Delhi – 110025, India

103 Penang Road, #05–06/07, Visioncrest Commercial, Singapore 238467

Cambridge University Press is part of Cambridge University Press & Assessment,
a department of the University of Cambridge.

We share the University's mission to contribute to society through the pursuit of
education, learning and research at the highest international levels of excellence.

www.cambridge.org
Information on this title: www.cambridge.org/9781009541992

DOI: 10.1017/9781009541961

First published 2025

A catalogue record for this publication is available from the British Library

ISBN 978-1-009-54199-2 Hardback
ISBN 978-1-009-54201-2 Paperback
ISSN 2753-6866 (online)
ISSN 2753-6858 (print)

Divination

A Cognitive Perspective

Elements in the Psychology of Religion

DOI: 10.1017/9781009541961
First published online: April 2025

Ze Hong
University of Macau

Author for correspondence: Ze Hong, zehong@um.edu.mo

Abstract: This Element adopts a naturalistic, cognitive perspective to understand divination. Following an overview of divination and the historical background of its scholarly study, Section 2 examines various definitions and proposes a working definition that balances common usage with theoretical coherence. Section 3 surveys existing theories of divination, including symbolic and functional perspectives, while critiquing their limitations. Section 4 argues for the primacy of cognition in divinatory practices, emphasizing the role of universal cognitive mechanisms and culturally specific worldviews in shaping their plausibility and persistence. Expanding on these ideas, Section 5 investigates the interplay between individual cognition and societal processes, highlighting sociocultural factors such as the preferential reporting of successful outcomes that bolster divination's perceived efficacy. Finally, Section 6 concludes by summarizing the Element's key arguments and identifying open questions for future research on the cognitive dimension of divination.

Keywords: divination, traditional belief systems, cognitive bias, worldview, ineffective technology

ISBNs: 9781009541992 (HB), 9781009542012 (PB), 9781009541961 (OC)
ISSNs: 2753-6866 (online), 2753-6858 (print)

Contents

1 Introduction

Divination, broadly understood as the practice of seeking knowledge of the unknown, holds significant importance and is prevalent across diverse human societies and throughout historical times. As a prominent anthropological subject, divination has been extensively documented and theorized by not only anthropologists but also historians (Johnston, 2009), psychologists (Smith, 2010), sociologists (Park, 1963), as well as scholars in the humanities and social sciences at large. The plethora of studies on divination, however, has been characterized by many inconsistencies: Divination has been described as intuitive (Struck, 2016) and deliberate (Kiernan, 1995), mystical (Saniotis, 2007) and empirical (Zeitlyn, 2021), and anxiety-relieving (Kuo & Kavanagh, 1994) and anxiety-inducing (Hong & Henrich, 2024) among other dichotomies. Some of these apparent inconsistencies are rhetorical, with scholars emphasizing what they consider under-researched aspects of divination or reacting against existing stereotypes. Yet at the same time, these contrasting characterizations also highlight the richness of divination, demonstrating its capacity to span a broad spectrum of diverse dimensions.

Much work has been devoted to examining the forms and functions of divination, and my goal in this Element is a modest one, with two specific aims. The first is to offer an up-to-date, naturalistic account of divination (in doing so I'll directly address its thorny definitional issue), and the second is to highlight why a cognitive approach is the most productive way of understanding divination. By "naturalistic account" I mean a theoretical framework that views divination as a natural product of human psychology and cultural transmission, free from the technical jargons that tend to mystify it,[1] and by "cognitive approach" I refer specifically to information production and individuals' mental processing of such information. Essentially, I advocate a "return to common sense" perspective by arguing that at its core, divination is what it appears to be: methods to generate information, usually to assist subsequent decision-making. Therefore, most divinatory practices are primarily cognitive activities and should be viewed as such (Hong & Henrich, 2021), and a key puzzle that this Element seeks to address is the persistence and recurrence of many divinatory practices that, from a modern scientific perspective, do not yield accurate information.

Divinatory practices have permeated human societies throughout history. From producing medicines to determining propitious moments for important

---

[1] This is unfortunately quite common in anthropology, such as "symbolic efficacy" (Langdon, 2007), ontological relativity" (Bråten, 2016), and "hermeneutics of suspicion" (Ringma & Brown, 1991).

events, humans frequently relied on signs or messages generated by the supernatural[2] (Karcher, 1998). The intellectual interest in divination can be traced back to ancient civilizations. Ancient Babylonian diviners explicitly theorized the possibility of divination in a causally interconnected universe (Annus, 2010); Plato thought of divination as a form of divine inspiration (Landry, 2014); Galen, the renowned medical practitioner of ancient Rome, considered medicine and divination as parallel arts while acknowledged divination's relevance in some medical matters (Van Nuffelen, 2014). Note that in explicit theorization of divination ancient scholars have also occasionally cast doubts on its validity. For instance, the famous orator of ancient Rome, Cicero, devoted an entire philosophical treatise *De Divinatione* (Cicero, 44 BCE/1921) questioning the rationale of Roman divination, and the Confucian scholar Xunzi explicitly expressed skepticism toward popular Chinese divination of his time (Lai, 2015).

During the colonial period, traditional forms of divination were described by Western travelers and missionaries as exotic cultural practices incompatible with Christianity (Silva, 2018). These early works mostly focused on the validity and legitimacy of divination with strong normative tones (i.e., whether divination is factually efficacious and/or morally permissible). In contrast, the intense scholarly interest in divination that arose in late nineteenth/early twentieth century Europe treated divination's objective ineffectiveness as a given and started to investigate the psychological, social, and cultural reasons for its persistence. This period also coincided with Europe's mounting intellectual interest in "primitive" [sic] societies, in particular their norms, customs, and rituals that were different from post-Enlightenment Europe (Barnard, 2021). Scholarly discussions on divination that occurred in both armchair theorizing and ethnographic writings during this time period typically subsumed divination into the larger category of magic or treated divination and magic as analogous cultural phenomena, and often offered explanations in cognitive terms. Tylor (1871), for example, implicitly treats divination, along with sorcery, witchcraft, "occult sciences," "black art" and other superstitions as magic, and describes it as parasitic, clinging to other, sounder information-generating methods; Frazer (1890) devotes an entire chapter on divination in his magnum opus *The Golden Bough* where he lays out his theory of sympathetic magic. Early ethnographers held similar views: Evans-Pritchard's (1937) classic ethnography on Azande explicitly discusses divination by feeding chickens poisons and observing whether they live or die (chicken oracle) in the context of

---

[2] This, of course, begs the question of what constitute as "supernatural." This thorny definitional issue will be discussed in subsequent sections.

magical practices with a thorough investigation of the reasoning processes behind such seemingly exotic practices. This way of interpreting indigenous religious beliefs and practices has been later termed "intellectualist" (Stocking Jr., 1986), meaning that it takes means-ends rationality seriously, and interprets such beliefs and practices as the applications of human beings' cognitive faculties to make sense of their world (Eames, 2016). Later theorists, however, gradually turned away from such positions, and have attempted to account for divination by placing it within evolutionist, diffusionist, ecological, or functionalist theories. Most of these theories rationalize divination after the fact, effectively removing it from the realm of intentional action (Tedlock, 2001).

The rise of symbolism and postmodernism in anthropology has led to a strong rejection of cognitive theories of magico-religious actions in general (Bloch, 2012; Jarvie, 2018), and divination has been interpreted as anything but attempts to obtain accurate information (Boyer, 2020). Granted, there is some heterogeneity in how anthropologists interpret divination, but the overall sentiment towards the cognitive approach is definitively negative (Hong & Henrich, 2024). Robin Horton, a vocal advocate for the intellectualist tradition, commented in 1967 that his thesis on African religious discourses as efforts to explain, predict, and control worldly events "has enjoyed a certain notoriety. Some few scholars have agreed enthusiastically with part or all of it. Others, more numerous, have been affronted ... All in all, the responses to the article have been predominantly unfavorable" (Horton, 1967). More recently, in a pointed critique of a *Current Anthropology* article advocating for a cognitive interpretation of divination (Matthews, 2022), prominent social anthropologist Holbraad sharply criticized the idea, stating: "if divination is indeed best understood as a technique for gaining information about the world ... it is an astonishingly bad one ... [therefore] taking diviners as putative providers of accurate information is plainly wrong."[3] Note that the rejection of the cognitive approach is also partly ideological: Because divination (and magic in general) does not achieve the ends it purports to achieve based on current scientific understanding of the world, to interpret such practices as genuine attempts at gaining accurate information or exerting influences on worldly events would mean that the indigenous people are mistaken, and in doing so the anthropologist would be implicitly accusing them of irrationality.[4]

---

[3] This argument is invalid because people everywhere can occasionally have norms and practices that are sub-optimal, often as a result of cultural transmission (Richerson & Boyd, 2005).

[4] Horton (1968) offers a similar argument for anthropologists in treating indigenous religious beliefs as explanation of this-worldly events (Horton himself considers this argument as mistaken): "Neo-Tylorians who take traditional beliefs at their face value therefore subscribe to the stereotype of the 'ignorant savage' and are illiberal racists. If on the other hand we treat them as having intentions which, despite appearances, are quite other than explanatory, we no longer have

While sociocultural anthropologists today have largely abandoned the cognitive approach, some researchers in psychology have taken an interest in seemingly irrational human beliefs and behaviors. Most psychological research in this area does not specifically target divination but focuses more broadly on the psychological mechanisms underpinning superstitions. In his much celebrated book *Believing in Magic: The Psychology of Superstition*, psychologist Stuart Vyse (1997) offers a comprehensive analysis of various types of superstitions in contemporary, modern societies. He posits that superstitions are the natural result of several well-understood psychological processes, including our sensitivity to coincidence, a penchant for developing rituals to fill time, our efforts to cope with uncertainty, the need for control, etc. This body of work builds upon decades of research on motivational and cognitive processes, most notably Kahneman and Tversky's work on cognitive biases and heuristics (Kahneman & Tversky, 1972, 1973; Tversky & Kahneman, 1973, 1974). For example, Vyse uses the availability heuristic to explain why people would consult an astrologer, numerologist, tarot-card reader, or psychic in the hope of finding out what their futures hold because of our frequent exposure to such practices in movies, television, and popular literature where their predictions were presented as genuinely accurate (Vyse, 1997, p. 241). Essentially, the pervasive presence of these cultural practices makes them readily accessible, skewing our perceptions towards believing in their efficacy. While biases and heuristics often provide important benefits – such as enabling swift, cost-efficient decision-making – they may occasionally lead us astray.

Other psychologists have adopted a more explicit evolutionary perspective. Rozin and colleagues (Nemeroff & Rozin, 2000; Rozin & Nemeroff, 1990, 2012a, 2012b) conducted a series of experimental studies that point to the adaptive benefits of sympathetic magical thinking. Their work suggests that the psychological mechanisms driving such thinking may have evolved because they offered significant survival and reproductive advantages to our ancestors. For instance, the aversion to objects that have been in contact with contaminants (what Frazer termed "contagious magic") could help avoid exposure to contagious microbes (Rozin & Nemeroff, 1990). More formally, evolutionary theorists have modeled the conditions under which superstitious behaviors may evolve, proposing that natural selection could favor strategies that lead to frequent errors in assessing causality between events as long as the occasional correct response carries a large fitness benefit (Foster & Kokko, 2009).

---

to evaluate traditional beliefs in the light of the canons of adequacy current in the sciences. Anthropologists who take this line are therefore not committed to the 'ignorant savage' stereotype. They are good liberals."

A related line of research, often associated with cognitive and evolutionary anthropology, explores how the forms of cultural practices contribute to their popularity and longevity within human populations. This body of work suggests that practices aligning with our evolved intuitions about the world are more likely to be favored over those that contradict them. According to this perspective, beliefs and practices persist in societies not only because they are true and effective – they often aren't – but more importantly because they *appear* to be true and effective. Singh (2022) refers to this as the "subjective selection" of culture, emphasizing the significance of our *subjective* assessment of cultural practices' utility, particularly actions aimed at achieving specific outcomes. An example often cited to illustrate this concept is bloodletting. This practice, which involves the extraction of blood to heal a patient, was a widespread and popular medical treatment both in the West and around the world for centuries (Kerridge & Lowe, 1995). However, we now understand that this practice generally did little to benefit the patient and, more often than not, was actually detrimental (Wootton, 2007). The question arises: What contributed to its recurrence and sustained its popularity for so long? Miton et al. (2015) suggest that there are cognitive mechanisms that predispose us to find the concept of bloodletting attractive. Specifically, humans have a strong intuition that good and bad things would go in and out of our body affecting health (Carey, 1985; Keil et al., 1999), which makes the idea that something bad coming out of the body would help illness recovery a plausible one. In a similar vein, Boyer (2020) argues that the success of many divination practices can be attributed to their "ostensive detachment," meaning that the methods used to obtain the verdict appear impartial and not influenced by the diviner's intentions or interests, thereby granting these practices more credibility than other sources of information whose content may be strategically manipulated by interested parties.

From these examples we can easily see how divination as a form of magic or superstition can be, and has been interpreted in cognitive terms. In general, cognitive approaches aim to address the puzzle of why we perceive causality where none exists (coincidentally, this was the question that early anthropologists like Tylor and Frazer sought to answer). Specifically, in the context of divination articulated in causal terms, the central question becomes: Why do humans believe that certain methods, protocols, or tools can "cause" the revelation of true and accurate information? It is important to note that cognitive theories of divination do not devalue other perspectives. Rather, as will be discussed in Section 4, the cognitive approach emphasizes the primacy of cognition in order to better understand the various functional aspects of divination.

The rest of this Element is organized as follows. I begin by exploring the various proposed definitions of divination and providing a working definition of divination that both respects its common usage and, as much as possible, maintains its theoretical coherence (Section 2). I then present a non-exhaustive survey of the existing theories of divination (Section 3) and lay out a detailed argument for the primacy of cognition in understanding divinatory practices (Section 4). Next, I examine the interplay between individual cognition and societal processes in reinforcing the credibility of divination in human populations (Section 5). Finally, I summarize the main points of the Element and highlight a few open questions that may merit future studies (Section 6).

2 Divination: The Thorny Definitional Issue

Social scientists do not always start their scholarly examinations of some subject by defining it (Swedberg, 2020). This is not because definitions are unimportant; rather it is often because offering a clear, useful, and comprehensive definition is difficult (Sørensen & Petersen, 2021). Such difficulty arises not only from the tension between the commonsense, folk understanding of a concept and its more technical, academic usage but also from the fact researchers across different disciplines often ascribe rather different meanings to the same term. Some notorious examples relevant to our discussion here include "religion" (Ferré, 1970; Guthrie, 1980; Horton, 1960; Jong, 2015), "ritual" (Goody, 1961; Snoek, 2006), and magic (Bremmer, 1999; Wax & Wax, 1963). Religion, for example, has been variously defined as the belief in spiritual beings (Tylor, 1871), systems to obtain welfare and avert misfortune (Hewitt, 1902), beliefs and practices that unite people into a single moral community (Durkheim, 1915), and anthropomorphism (Guthrie, 1980), among others. To date, no scholarly consensus has been reached on a single definition. Partly as a result, efforts to analytically distinguish religion from other cultural practices such as magic (Frazer, 1890; Thomas, 2003) have not been successful, leading to the adoption of the compromise term "magico-religious."

So why bother with a definition at all? Indeed, there have always been suggestions to dispense with overarching concepts such as "religion" (Jong, 2015; Nadel, 1954), and it is perhaps better to understand religion as a polythetic term denoting such diverse phenomena that they cannot be situated under a single explanatory theory (Boyer, 1994; Nordin, 2023). While I fully acknowledge the difficulties in coming up with coherent definitions for complex human cultural phenomena that would satisfy everyone, the cost of abandoning the definitional effort altogether seems too great.

In a discussion of the necessity of defining religion in anthropology, Horton (1960) gives two reasons for the importance of definitions. First, for many nonanthropologists the term "religion" carries a clear connotation and anthropologists have the duty to engage with and theorize such folk understandings.[5] More crucially, however, he asserts:

> To go ahead with the comparative study of religion while leaving the scope of the term undefined is to behave in a self-stultifying way, for until some fairly precise criteria of inclusion of phenomena in the denotation of "religion" have been given, it is impossible to specify those variables whose behavior we have to try to explain in our study.

While Horton's comments specifically target the "comparative study of religion," his argument extends broadly to social scientific research. Without shared definitions, scholars are left without a common ground, leading to fragmented and possibly contradictory findings and making incremental progress difficult. Lacking a definition for a general concept X precludes the development of a general theory, as it remains unclear whether a specific variable x could be applied or tested against the theory. Additionally, without a clear definition, measuring X becomes impractical, as it is impossible to determine whether x qualifies as X, and precise measurement has become key in nearly all empirical scientific endeavors (Hand, 2004; Muller, 2018).

Fortunately, our discussion here is not about religion. Nonetheless, as I will show, defining "divination" proves to be similarly challenging. Like religion, a thorough discussion of definition is important because 1) both scholars and lay people have (sometimes strong) intuitions of what divination means, 2) marking the boundaries of what does and does not count as divination affects how we theorize the psychological/cognitive factors and social mechanisms that contribute to the rise and persistence of divinatory practices, and 3) a clear definition of divination can help us understand different theories of divination and why scholars sometimes talk past each other. Let's begin by examining some standard dictionary definitions:

> The action or practice of divining; the foretelling of future events or discovery of what is hidden or obscure by supernatural or magical means; soothsaying, augury, prophecy. (Oxford English Dictionary)

---

[5] One could make similar arguments for the need to communicate with other disciplines in academia. As Sørensen and Petersen (2021) suggests, "disciplines that abandon too many of their once cherished categories ... risk being disconnected from the wider metabolism of the scientific community, as neighboring disciplines cannot always be bothered to invest huge amount of energy to redefine or replace categories."

> The art or practice that seeks to foresee or foretell future events or discover hidden knowledge usually by the interpretation of omens or by the aid of supernatural powers (Merriam-Webster Dictionary)

These definitions are largely in line with those found in scholarly writings when the subject matter is explicitly defined. For example, divination has been defined as "the foretelling of future events or discovery of what is hidden or obscure by supernatural or magical means" (Fiskesjo, 2001), "a way of exploring the unknown in order to elicit answers to questions beyond the range of ordinary human understanding" (Tedlock, 2001), or practices "to discover what is hidden by 'supernatural' or irrational means, to see things through 'magical' insight" (Karcher, 1998). One can easily see that the common theme of these definitions is that divination is an information-generating practice characterized as "supernatural," "magical," or "beyond ordinary," with the implicit assumption that readers are already familiar with these qualifying adjectives. These terms serve to categorize information-generating practices[6] into two distinct types: the natural and ordinary versus the supernatural and extraordinary. This categorization leads to the immediate follow-up question: What exactly do "supernatural," "magical," and "beyond ordinary" mean? Addressing this proves to be a complex task.

To address these definitional challenges, I propose a typology of divination with two categories: a "narrow sense," referring specifically to systematic rituals that interpret signs or patterns believed to involve some form of divine agency, and a "broad sense," encompassing any cultural practice for obtaining information that appears implausible by contemporary scientific standards. This distinction accommodates the wide variability of practices termed "divination" across cultures while maintaining analytical clarity. The following discussion will explore how these definitions emerge from the considerations outlined in this section and why they are analytically superior to other definitions for framing divination within a cognitive framework.

2.1 "Supernatural" as a Qualifier

Let us begin by revisiting traditional attempts to define divination through its non-ordinary nature. Taking "supernatural" as an example (with other qualifiers following a similar logic), we immediately encounter the question of whether to define it emically (from an insider's perspective) or etically (from an outsider's perspective). Mainstream anthropological thinking often privileges the emic approach of adopting the native's point of view, but this approach is problematic with the concept of the "supernatural" because it likely does not exist in many

---

[6] Similar problem arises when defining magic; see Wax and Wax (1963).

cultures.[7] There have been heated discussions in anthropology regarding whether the supernatural constitutes a valid emic category (Dein, 2016; Lohmann, 2003; Winzeler, 2012), in particular whether the natural versus supernatural dichotomy is a Western construct imposed on many traditional, small-scale societies (Hallowell, 1960). A cursory look at the ethnographic literature reveals much direct commentary on the lack of natural versus supernatural distinction in premodern, non-Western societies: "few preindustrial cultures make a neat distinction between natural and supernatural phenomena ... [as they] ... may simply lack emic categories for 'natural' and 'supernatural'" (Petrus & Bogopa, 2007); "our use of the notion "supernatural" does not correspond to any Gururumba concept: they do not divide the world into natural and supernatural parts" (Newman, 1965, p. 83); "supernatural persons ... [if applied to characters in the myths of the northern Ojibwa] ... is completely misleading, if for no other reason than the fact that the concept of 'supernatural' presupposes a concept of the 'natural.' The latter is not present in Ojibwa thought" (Hallowell, 1960). In his masterpiece *Witchcraft, oracles and magic among the Azande*, Evans-Pritchard (1937) similarly makes the following comment on the lack of the natural versus supernatural distinction of the Azande people:

> To us supernatural means very much the same as abnormal or extraordinary. Azande certainly have no such notions of reality. They have no conception of 'natural' as we understand it, and therefore neither of the 'supernatural' as we understand it. Witchcraft is to Azande an ordinary and not an extraordinary, even though it may in some circumstances be an infrequent, event. It is a normal, and not an abnormal happening.

Of course, we need to approach these ethnographic accounts with caution, mindful of ethnographers' biases and the selective nature of their reporting (Geertz, 1973). We should also bear in mind that there are accounts pointing to the opposite: Malinowski, for example, suggests that the Trobriand islanders may indeed have the emic concept of "supernatural"[8] and would apply magical and rational means selectively to achieve desired outcomes in different

---

[7] Typically, anthropologists use the term "emic" to describe concepts that are explicit in the culture, and it's likely that there are important implicit concepts (e.g., those regarding the supernatural) as well. Here, I intend to use "emic" to refer to both types of concepts, and suggest that the concept of "supernatural" as a qualitatively different type of ontological category from the "natural" likely do not exist in many societies.

[8] To be sure, Malinowski uses the word "supernatural" in a rather loose manner and never bothers to define it. However, in numerous occasions in his writings, Malinowski suggests that "natural" and "supernatural" are valid categories from the indigenous point of view, for example, "primitive man recognizes both the natural and the supernatural forces and agencies, and he tries to use them both for his benefit." (Malinowski, 1992)

situations (Malinowski, 1992). However, the overwhelming consensus from these ethnographic descriptions is that many societies do not explicitly recognize the distinction between natural and supernatural, and the concept of the "supernatural" often does not constitute a valid emic category. Indeed, early social theorists like Durkheim have posited that the notion of the supernatural is relatively recent in the history of human thought, emerging alongside the rise of Enlightenment science in the seventeenth and eighteenth centuries (Durkheim, 1915). Thus, for the vast majority of human history, the world was mostly viewed as an integrated whole, without clear divisions between different ontological realms[9] (Sahlins, 2022).

We are then left with the etic approach, but defining the supernatural in etic perspectives is not without problems, either. For one thing, the modern Western understanding of "supernatural" is far from clear-cut (Saler, 1977). Delineating the meaning of the term can involve sophisticated theological discussions on the nature of reality (Berger, 1977), and its usage by social scientists is similarly ambiguous, as it is often used as a convenient shorthand to refer to a broad cluster of loosely related phenomena and events. A systematic review of psychologists' employment of "supernatural" and related terms by Lindeman and Svedholm (2012) reveals that these concepts are variably defined as either domain-general (e.g., false beliefs, scientifically impossible phenomena, associative biases, irrational acts) or domain-specific (e.g., specific beliefs that violate our intuitive ontology). The authors conclude that domain-general definitions are problematic because they are either too narrow (e.g., associative bias does not encompass belief in devils) or too broad (e.g., false beliefs would include the belief that dolphins are fish which does not appear supernatural), and propose that supernatural beliefs are best described as a confusion of ontological categories, that is, misattributing properties that belong to objects/events in one category to those in another category. For example, this can include beliefs that thoughts can move external objects or that force or energy can possess life (e.g., Feng Shui, Chi), as well as the idea that minds can exist independently of bodies and operate as animate entities (e.g., angels, devils, and ghosts).

The examination of the definitional issue of "supernatural" has two important implications for our discussion of divination. Firstly, it highlights the need for an etic approach in defining divination, one that leans on a scientific understanding of the world and its causal structures. Secondly, we must recognize that the use of the term "supernatural" – along with similar terms like "occult," "obscure," or "non-ordinary" – is not without its complications. As I will argue,

---

[9] This, of course, does not mean people do not recognize that gods and mortals are different types of entities. Rather, the idea here is that people's attitudes (in the sense of Van Leeuwen (2014)) towards these entities are qualitatively the same.

while Lindeman and Svedholm's (2012) definition of "supernatural" makes it a good qualifier for "magic," it requires some adjustments to suitably apply to "divination."

2.2 Demarcating Divination from Non-divination and the Two Senses of Divination

As with most complex sociocultural phenomena, any general theory of divination faces a demarcation problem. In her book *Ancient Greek Divination*, Sarah Johnston (2009, p. 5) explicitly points this out:

> The good diviner knew about the sympathetic links between, say, the appearance of a night-owl during the day and political insurrection and could therefore predict what was going to happen when such a bird showed up. But this prompted such questions as how we should distinguish between the art of the diviner and the art of the doctor, the farmer, the sailor or anyone else who made it his business to learn how one thing signified another that was yet to come – is it divination to know that an olive crop will be abundant by looking at blooms early in the season, or is that just good arboriculture? Is it divination to predict rain by looking at a dark cloud, or is that simply the sort of practical meteorology that every reasonably intelligent person picks up during the course of life?

Now, if we remind ourselves of the dictionary definition of divination, can we say in any sense that the use of dark clouds to predict rainfall is natural while the use of a night owl to predict a political insurrection is supernatural? One way to make the distinction is to appeal to the involvement of the divine, as Johnston herself seems to suggest: If the signs are believed to be provided by (typically anthropomorphized) deities, then the method of interpreting these signs may be deemed divination. After all, the etymological root of "divination" has an unambiguous link to the idea of divine involvement, a concept frequently assumed, either explicitly or implicitly, within scholarly discussions (Brown, 2006; Zuesse, 1975). In discussing the status of prophecy as a possible form of divination, for example, Kitz (2003) explicitly states the "fundamental principle" of divination: " ... divination is based on one very simple premise: all divine action causes material reaction." Thus, divination can be viewed as a practice of communicating with anthropomorphized superhuman entities such as Gods, spirits, or deceased ancestors.[10] Throughout this Element, I will label this "divination as communication with the divine" as the "narrow-sense" definition of divination.

---

[10] Such narrow-sense definition traces back to ancient times; Sextus, for example, explicitly emphasizes the "divine" component: "If there are no gods, then there can be no divination, since divination is "the science which observes and interprets the signs given by gods to men," not in any of its forms, inspiration, astrology, hepatoscopy, or oneiromancy." (Hankinson, 1988)

This definition aligns well with Tylor's (1871) minimal definition of religion as a belief in spiritual beings, offering the benefits of precision and elegance. However, defining divination in this narrow sense would leave out many practices that do not invoke any superhuman agent yet are traditionally recognized as forms of divination, both in ancient and modern contexts such as *Yijing* (*I Ching*), tarot cards, and palm reading.[11] This calls for the formulation of a "broad-sense" definition of divination, one that encompasses these practices while simultaneously distinguishing them from ordinary information technology.

Let's refine the use of the term "supernatural" to better suit our purposes. Lindeman and Svedholm (2012) define the supernatural as mistaking ontological categories – an etic perspective, since practitioners and believers likely do not view their beliefs as mistaken. While this approach works fine for magic, it doesn't fully encompass broad-sense divination, which is fundamentally rooted in a belief in the interconnectedness of the universe (French, 2005, p. 135; Hong, 2024), often contradicting our current scientific understanding of worldly causality. This notion bears resemblance to the concept of "ontological category confusion" but extends beyond it by positing causal links between events and phenomena that do not necessarily belong to different ontological categories yet are unrelated from the perspective of modern science (Hong & Henrich, 2021). Consider the use of astrology to predict personal outcomes, based on the assumption that the positions and movements of celestial bodies influence human lives. This belief does not conflate ontological categories, as both celestial entities and human experiences exist within the physical world. Yet, it posits a causal relationship deemed implausible by our current (scientific) understanding of the world due to the absence of known mechanisms linking the two types of entities. As such, "supernatural" in this context signifies more than mere incorrect beliefs; it refers to beliefs in causal relationships lacking any scientifically plausible mechanism. Conversely, some cultural practices are based on factually incorrect beliefs but are not typically categorized as divination.

Let us consider fetal sex prediction as an example to illustrate how the proposed demarcation scheme works in practice. In modern societies, ultrasound technology can determine fetal sex with nearly 100 percent accuracy, and no one would consider it divination – its legitimacy is firmly grounded in the scientific understanding of biology and physics. More interesting are the various "folk" methods of fetal sex prediction. On one hand, some methods deviate significantly from our modern understanding of causality. For example, popular numerological methods in China calculate fetal sex based on the mother's age and the month of

---

[11] Boyer (2020) gives a number of examples of divinatory practices in which superhuman agents are not believed to be involved, and also notes that there could be substantial heterogeneity in lay people's understanding of

conception (Hong & Zinin, 2023), and the use of dreams to foretell a baby's sex is a recurring belief in many traditional societies (Hong, 2022b). Under the proposed demarcation scheme, these methods would be classified as "divination" because they are scientifically implausible. On the other hand, there are methods, such as associating maternal food cravings or abdominal bumps with fetal sex, that appear biologically plausible but do not perform better than chance (Forbes, 1959; Hong & Zinin, 2023). In this framework, these biologically plausible but scientifically unsupported methods would not qualify as "divination." To drive the point home, consider the use of fundal height to predict fetal sex. While its predictive validity is highly questionable, I trust that most readers would intuitively agree that it does not belong in the category of "divination."

Figure 1 shows a general topology of divinatory practices in this framework. To reiterate, "narrow-sense" divination refers to communication with the divine (anthropomorphized superhuman deities), and in accordance with the existing literature, I differentiate between two primary methods of divination: inspired divination, where the diviner directly receives and communicates information from a deity, often as a specific message, and technical divination, which involves the diviner interpreting the hidden meanings behind natural occurrences, signs, or omens[12] (Flower, 2008; Kitz, 2003). This is an ancient classification which traces at least back to Plato, who famously expressed

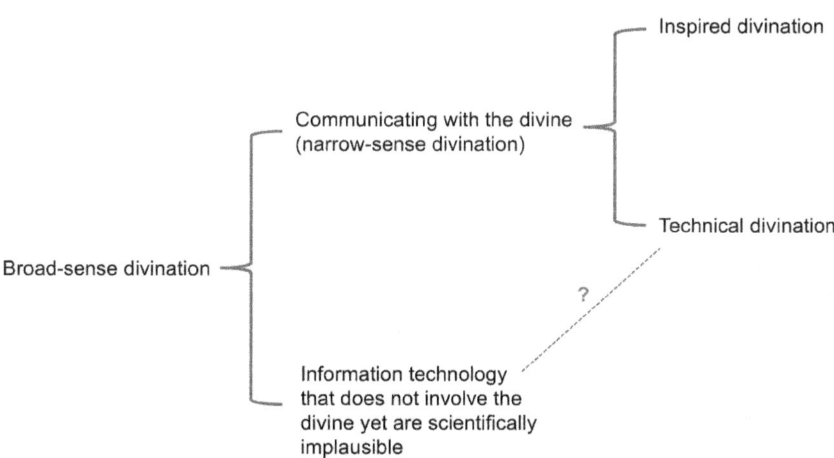

Figure 1 A typology of divination practices.

---

[12] This dichotomy has been variously termed possession/intuitive/direct vs. mechanical/inductive/ artificial. Confusingly, Cicero refers to the former kind as "natural" divination (Denyer, 1985), which highlights the importance for modern scholars to be cautious about their use of natural/ supernatural to categorize divinatory practices.

a preference for inspired divination, arguing that human interpretations of divine signs are inherently prone to errors and misjudgments (Landry, 2014).

Broad-sense divination, on the other hand, includes both narrow-sense divination and scientifically implausible information technology that does not involve communication with the divine. There has been some inconsistency in whether to classify the latter kind of divination as "technical divination" (illustrated by a dashed line with a question mark in Figure 1), and I have no intention of policing the scholarly usage of divination here. I do, however, wish to highlight the implicit assumption of "divination as implausible information technology" in contemporary scholarly discourse. Phrenology, for example, has often been referred to as a form of "divination" by modern scholars (Robertson, 2018). Anthropologists also sometimes use the term "divination" pejoratively to critique what they view as questionable, in particular ethically problematic information technologies, such as genetic testing (Lock, 2005; Palmié, 2007) and big data/algorithmic predictions (Cabrera, 2020; Lazaro, 2023).

This topology is a decidedly etic approach[13] that aims to capture its usage within (Western) academic discourse. Although not a "carving nature by its joints" way of demarcating divination from non-divination, it provides an analytically useful framework for understanding various cognitive and social factors influencing different types of divinatory practices. Such a definition of divination also implies that whether we categorize a particular information-generating technology as divination hinges on the perceived presence of a scientifically plausible mechanism linking the sign and the outcome, rather than its empirical record of predictive success and failures. Indeed, an intuitive understanding of the validity of technological practices often precedes the need for "data" (Hong & Henrich, 2021).

3 Theories of Divination

As mentioned in the introduction, divination stands out as a prominent cultural practice in many human societies and has attracted much scholarly attention. Because it is often implicitly seen as implausible forms of information technology in contemporary scholarly discourse,[14] numerous theories have been proposed to explain its prevalence and recurrence in human societies I wish to

---

[13] Some scholars have suggested that divination is viewed by both the practitioner and observer as a special way of gaining knowledge (Sørensen, 2021). I am skeptical of the "special" status attributed to divination compared to ordinary information technology for the same reasons regarding the applicability of "supernatural" as a valid emic category in many traditional societies.

[14] See Park (1963): "In a general way, diviners are to be classed with the native herbalist and the shaman as private practitioners of an art to which natural science lends little support . . . reason would seem to suggest that on the whole he is likely to do as much harm as good."

emphasize that, according to the definition I just offered, divination is "implausible" only from a modern scientific perspective – not for the diviners and clients themselves. For those engaging in these practices, divinatory techniques are typically perceived as highly plausible, making their use entirely rational within their cultural and cognitive frameworks.

Among the proposed theories, symbolic and functional approaches are particularly notable, and they will be the focus of this section. Symbolist approaches in anthropology suggest that divinatory practices are rarely what they appear to be; rather, they symbolize something else, and it is the job of anthropologists to discover their hidden meaning (Douglas, 1975; Turner, 1975). Functional explanations additionally emphasize their functions either at the individual or the societal level, with societal functions frequently aimed at bolstering social solidarity and cohesion (Jarvie, 1986). Note that scholars do not always explicitly define divination in their analysis, sometimes using the term "divination" in rather idiosyncratic ways. Thus, these theories are not exhaustive explanations of divination, a caveat often acknowledged by the authors themselves. In the ensuing discussion, I will briefly outline these theoretical frameworks with concrete examples, and then in the next section argue that while symbolic and functional theories provide valid insights into divination, they ultimately rest on a cognitive foundation to offer coherent explanations of human behavior.

3.1 Divination as Dispute Resolution

A common way in which divination has been explained is mechanism for resolving disputes. This perspective posits divination as an arbitrative tool to facilitate agreement in challenging situations (Johnston, 2005). For example, Victor Turner (1968) highlights divination's role in social redress among the Ndembu people. According to Turner, Ndembu diviners try to elicit from their clients' responses which give them clues to the current tensions in their groups. Divination, in this case, becomes a form of social analysis that reveals hidden conflicts so that they can be dealt with by institutional norms and procedures. Turner notes that diviners, through experience, have learned to "reduce their social system to a few basic principles and factors, and to juggle with these until they arrive at a decision that accords with the view of the majority of the clients at any given consultation" (p. 51). Furthermore, the public nature of divination, especially in emotionally charged contexts, allows diviners to reaffirm social norms in impactful ways. Similarly, Park (1963) argues that the people employ divination in the selection of a house site in which "the diviner in effect provides a legitimating sanction upon a process of structural realignment which . . . would be difficult indeed to sanction in any remarkably different manner." According to Park, selecting a house site influences not only the actor him/herself but also their kinship network, and involves the important decision of whether or not to stay with or depart from one's kinship network. In this scenario, divination "depersonalizes" an otherwise deeply personal and impactful decision and thus precludes potential disputes and conflicts.

Another prominent cultural phenomenon that falls into the category of dispute resolution that involves the divine is trial by ordeal, in which God(s) is/are believed to condemn the guilty and exonerate the innocent through formally conducted physical tests (Radding, 1979). Trial by ordeal itself was rather ancient and has been suggested to have existed as early as the time of Hammurabi in ancient Babylon (Bell, 2017), and has been extensively studied by legal scholars (Gross, 1937; Kamali, 2018). Though not always classified as divination in the literature, trial by ordeal fits nicely in the topology of divination in Section 2 as a way of determining the guilt/innocence of suspects with the help of the divine. The specific methods of ordeal can vary, but the general idea is that if the suspect is able to go through the tests unharmed, then they are proven innocent as God is on their side (Leeson, 2012). Various theories have been proposed to explain this seeming irrationality, and functional approaches (particularly in legal scholarships) emphasize the role trial by ordeal plays in forming consensus and unity in communities. Hyams (1981), for example, suggests that trial by ordeal in medieval England often served to release tensions and reinforce the community's standards of proper behavior by having God publicly cast his judgment. Bartlett (1986) similarly argues that ordeal was a reasonable instrument for settling disputes in medieval Europe, and it was mostly used in extraordinary situations when other modes of proof failed. Trial by ordeal, or more broadly the invocation of the divine to help distinguish the guilty and the innocent similarly exists in many traditional societies, in particular in the context of identifying witchcraft and sorcery (Evans-Pritchard, 1937; Hiltunen, 1986; Lambert, 1956).

3.2 Divination as Mechanism to Legitimize Political Power

In societies with complex political hierarchies, divination is often a highly political matter and under tight regulations of the state (Cooley et al., 2014; Pecírková, 1985; Smith, 1986). As such, a common functional interpretation of divination in these contexts is that it helps legitimize and solidify political power. For example, elaborate divination procedures in the Shang and Zhou dynasties of ancient China were argued to support the bureaucratic institutions as a source of state power (Flad, 2008), and ancient Mesopotamian kings often employed professional diviners who would offer favorable interpretations of existing omens regarding the kings' rule out of political expediency (Brown, 2006).

A particularly noteworthy form of divination is celestial (or astral) divination, where heavenly phenomena are believed to be associated with earthly (political) affairs (Reiner, 1995; Swerdlow, 1999). Historically, this form of divination was frequently employed to justify the legitimacy of the rulers of the state by showing auspicious signs from Heaven. A memorable example occurred in ancient Rome, where the appearance of a comet in 44 BCE, shortly after the assassination of Julius Caesar, was interpreted by many Romans as a sign of Caesar's deification. Augustus (then Octavian) used this celestial event to bolster his political position by claiming that the comet was Caesar's soul ascending to the heavens, thereby implying divine favor for himself as Caesar's heir (Gurval, 1997).

A more salient political use of divine messages is perhaps oneiromancy, the deciphering of dreams to extract meaningful information. In traditional China, dreams of suns and dragons were typically associated with imperial power, and historical records have shown a plethora of instances where princes and other competitors to the throne used (or fabricated) such dreams to enhance political legitimacy (Hong, 2022b; Yu, 2022), and historians similarly had an incentive to retrospectively fabricate such dreams to justify the emperors' political power of their own dynasty (Fang, 2015). For example, the official dynastic record of the Eastern Han Dynasty documented a story of its founding father, the Guangwu Emperor, recounting a dream to one of his generals as he was achieving tremendous military success yet had not officially declared himself emperor:

> 'Last night I dreamed of myself riding a red dragon flying into the sky; when I woke up, my heart beat real fast.' Feng Yi (a military general) said: 'This is your soul induced/moved by the Heavenly Mandate. The unrest in your heart is due to your habitual prudence.' Then he started to discuss with other generals on officially proposing Guangwu to be the emperor. (Hou Hanshu, chapter 17)

As modern readers, we cannot know exactly whether Guangwu indeed had such a dream or was merely fabricating it, but its political significance is obvious. In a cultural context where dreams were believed to be a valid channel for divine messages, it is no surprise that political actors strategically resort to it for their own advantage. More generally, divinatory signs could be used as political arguments for persuasion purposes (Hong & Chen, 2024; Ramsey, 2023). In the Neo-Assyrian period, for example, royal advisors often counseled their kings using the celestial omen series (Rochberg, 2004, p. 220).

3.3 Divination as a Method to Reduce Uncertainty and Alleviate Anxiety

Of course, divination does not always occur in the public and may be utilized in rather private settings, particularly where its usage is deemed illegitimate by the authorities,[15] or when the information sought is highly personal. Scholars have also offered individual-level explanations, the most common being that divination helps alleviate anxiety by reducing uncertainty[16] in what appears chaotic and mysterious. Such examples are widespread across different historical contexts. Professional dream interpreters, for instance, were believed to alleviate the anxiety of worried rulers in traditional China by clarifying the meaning of otherwise vague dreams (Vance, 2017), and ancient Greek divination has been described as a "cultural heuristic to help people overcome the unpleasant feelings of uncertainty and the fear of the unknown" (Jouan, 1990). In the context of decision-making where clients desperately need practical information to handle pressing matters, divination can also be used to directly guide actions, thereby relieving the clients' anxiety. This type of explanation often emphasizes the reduction of psychological discomfort as a result of the reduction of uncertainty, and implies that the participants in divination understand that their efforts do not "work" in a tangible sense. Instead, divination primarily provides psychological comfort in situations where no other solution is available. This line of thinking traces back to Malinowski's analysis of magic, where he suggests that people recognize the limits of their empirical knowledge and capacity, yet are driven by strong emotional factors such as anxiety, fears, and hopes when they resort to magic (Malinowski, 1992). In other words, magic functions to preserve human confidence (even if illusory) in threatening situations (Kippenberg, 1997).

Such explanations, which focus on individuals' psychological needs for certainty and control, are also common in the anthropological literature, and often have an added dimension of "meaning-making." Victor Turner (the same author that describes divination as dispute resolution), in his analysis of divination in rural Africa, highlights that in harsh environments with high morbidity and mortality rates, low nutritional levels, plagues, droughts, and famines, diviners can counteract the fears and anxieties produced by such indeterminacy though the frequent interposition of their overdetermined schemata provided by divination, which restores coherence and meaning. (Turner, 1975, p. 25).

---

[15] Early Christians, for example, often viewed magic and divination as illegal and/or immoral (Coy, 2016).

[16] There are many ways in which divination can simplify complex and chaotic patterns. Traditional Chinese numerology, for example, is famous for uncertainty reduction through computation (Homola, 2019; Matthews, 2021).

Similarly, Denham (2015) gives the following description of Nankani (an ethnic group in Northern Ghana) divination that involves seeking answers from ancestral spirits:

> During divination sessions, the client works between their reflective self and their idealized conception of the ancestors. This split is not pathological, but a useful and culturally derived method for the management or reduction of existential anxiety, changing social relations, and uncertain circumstances. Divination and, in particular, the divinatory selfscape that emerges, mediates this split and assists in resolving uncertainty and generating meaning.

This particular account emphasizes the role divination plays in making sense of the apparently unexplainable (e.g., "Why does this misfortune happen to me?"), and even if there are no immediate action recommendations, obtaining a coherent and sensible explanation could confer affective benefits. Other scholars have explicitly emphasized the therapeutic effect of divination (Ajala, 2013; Bohannan, 1975; Zempléni, 1975); in fact, divination sessions have sometimes been compared to modern psychological counseling (Chuang, 2011; Kohol & Akuto, 2019).

Some psychologists similarly suggest that a psychological need to relieve anxiety may be a sufficient explanation for certain types of divination (Jahoda, 1970). While studies in psychology are typically not about divination per se, there have been a number of studies on how the need for psychological certainty contributes to superstitious thinking and behaviors generally. Baseball players, for example, are suggested to be particularly superstitious due to the inherent risks and uncertainties in their games. These superstitions often manifest themselves in the form of routinized rituals that may be idiosyncratic to individual players (Gmelch, 2010). The literature on pathological gambling also frequently invokes cognitive biases such as the illusion of control to account for superstitious behaviors in games with significant uncertainty (Cocker & Winstanley, 2015; Griffiths, 1990). Similarly, theories such as compensatory control propose that individuals employ "compensatory strategies" to manage uncertainty – such as affiliating with external systems perceived to act on their behalf or seeking out simple, clear, and consistent interpretations of the social and physical environment – to regain a sense of control over their lives (Landau et al., 2015). Unlike anthropological approaches, psychological perspectives typically assume that individuals might genuinely hold false beliefs due to faulty reasoning – a point we will revisit – and that these beliefs lead to tangible behavioral consequences.

3.4 Divination as a Special Way of Knowing

Though functional and individual-psychological theories of divination currently dominate the scholarly discourse, there have been attempts to describe divination as a special way of knowing (Tedlock, 2001). These accounts are "cognitive" in so far as the authors are dissatisfied with functional accounts of divination that emphasize only their sociopolitical aspects or anxiety-relieving /therapeutic effects, and call for greater attention to the practice of divination itself as an information-generating activity. Divination is "special," however, in that this kind of knowing is to be distinguished from ordinary information technology.

A recent account that attempts to explain divination in informational terms concerns how it helps us express intuitions. The idea itself was quite novel[17] when the classicist Peter Struck (2016) offered a comprehensive account with an elaborate analysis of how ancient Greek employed divination for such a purpose, and there have been a few follow-up studies since (Baratz, 2022). According to Struck, divination does not produce new information in a technical sense but serves to uncover and convey knowledge already held subconsciously. In cognitive science, it is well established that we know certain things without understanding how (Gigerenzer, 2007; Radman, 2012), and divination is "the most robust ancient version in a long series of attempts" to express this "surplus knowledge" (Struck, 2016, p. 15). Struck argues at length that ancient philosophers often attributed sudden, inexplicable insights to divine sources, and this type of involuntary, gut-feeling sort of knowledge parallels the modern concept of cognitive intuition. Note that Struck labels his approach "cognitive," as clearly seen in the title of his book *Divination and Human Nature: A Cognitive History of Intuition in Classical Antiquity*. By "cognitive" he means that divination, especially inspired divination, can be viewed as a method of acquiring information through intuition rather than rational inference or conscious deliberation.

More generally, divination is sometimes suggested to operate as a "non-normal" mode of cognition (Peek, 1991). Spirit possession in shamanism exemplifies this, where diviners enter altered states of consciousness (Beattie & Middleton, 1969). Anthropologists generally accept the sincerity of the diviners (i.e., that they are not charlatans merely faking it) in these contexts, and there is plenty of evidence showing that professional shamans do genuinely seek to enter altered states and sometimes would resort to the use of hallucinogenic plants and other psychedelics (Hatsis, 2018; Metzner, 1998).

---

[17] though there had been some anthropological allusions; see Tedlock (2001) and Silva (2014).

A feature of many anthropological accounts that suggest divination as a special way of knowing is their somewhat elusive and ambiguous stance on the truth status (in the ordinary sense) of information generated by divination and the motivations behind individuals engaging in it (Hong & Henrich, 2024). Some examples include " ... [divination] is itself a mode of discovery that makes a truth-claim with regard to how it represents the world ... the diviners' claims are incommensurate with those of anthropologists" (Myhre, 2006), "The role of the truths that diviners pronounce is not to make a claim about the world but rather to change it – to interfere, in other words, in its ontological constitution" (Holbraad, 2009), "within the divinatory space, past experience and potential futures are brought together, framed by the querent's current questions and needs and interpreted through the lens of the present. In doing so, the authentic is resituated; it is not linear but experiential ... " (Sawden, 2018). I submit that these statements can be challenging to comprehend even for professional social scientists, let alone readers without much expertise in recent theoretical developments in anthropology (e.g., postmodernism and the ontological turn). The basic point is really that while divination seeks to generate information, it is not concerned with truth in the correspondence sense – where the truth or falsity of a statement is determined by how accurately it describes the world.[18] This is why Holbraad (2019) claims that Cuban divination always produces truth by emphasizing the transformative aspect of divination, that divination is "indubitable" because divinatory statements are not merely (or even primarily) representations of the world but help the client reconstruct her experiences in her particular contexts.

4 A "Commonsense" Cognitive Approach and Why Cognition Serves as the Foundation to Understand Divination

Having introduced several major theories of divination, I now turn to an approach that, in my view, has not received sufficient attention in the scholarly literature. While scholars such as Devisch (2013) have made significant contributions by classifying various theories of divination, I find the distinction between symbolic/functional perspectives and cognitive ones particularly helpful. This distinction not only underscores the importance of cognition but also highlights the differences between the cognitive approach I advocate (which I will discuss in subsequent sections) and the cognitive approaches addressed in the previous section.

---

[18] More broadly, the correspondence theory of truth is the view of the truth value of statements depends only on its correspondence with the objective reality. For a comprehensive philosophical introduction, see (David, 2022).

As mentioned in the introduction, I argue that divination is primarily a cognitive activity and should be viewed as such, and in this regard I am on the side of scholars discussed in Section 3.4. However, I further argue that divination as an "epistemic technology" is not qualitatively different from ordinary information-generating methods and they could be (and should be) theorized within a general framework for understanding human technologies (Hong & Henrich, 2021). More explicitly, my proposed "commonsense" approach views divination as fundamentally a cognitive activity aimed at generating information to reduce uncertainty and guide decision-making. In other words, people resort to divination because they seek accurate information about matters of pragmatic interest, typically to inform decisions. This approach emphasizes three core principles:

1) Instrumentality of Divination: Divination is primarily understood as an epistemic tool – an information-generating practice that individuals use to address unknowns or uncertainties in their lives. This perspective takes seriously the ways in which participants, whether diviners or clients, approach divination as a means to obtain actionable insights, regardless of whether the outcomes align with empirical reality.

2) Cognitive Mechanisms: The efficacy and persistence of divination are underpinned by universal cognitive mechanisms such as pattern recognition, causal reasoning, and decision-making heuristics. These mechanisms help explain why divinatory practices appear plausible and useful to their practitioners, even when they do not conform to scientific understandings of causality.

3) Contextual and Social Dynamics: While rooted in individual cognition, divination practices are shaped and reinforced by social and cultural contexts, especially in the process of information transmission. Factors such as worldview and preferential reporting of successful outcomes contribute to the perceived validity and credibility of divination in different societies.

In what follows I will first provide evidence for the instrumentality of divination, that is, humans primarily take divination as a means to obtain accurate information, then explain why functional accounts of divination require a cognitive basis, and finally synthesize existing work on the psychological and cognitive factors that sustain belief in divination.

4.1 Ethnographic and Historical Evidence for the Instrumentality of Divination

Few would deny that, at face value, the objective of divination appears to be obtaining information. Yet as I have mentioned, many (especially anthropological) accounts of divination have maintained that divination is not really about know-ledge acquisition but rather aims to uncover the deeper meaning or hidden function of divination. While these perspectives offer valuable insights, they sometimes overlook or misinterpret the substantial ethnographic and historical evidence that underscores the face-value instrumentality of divination. It's evident not only in how diviners market their services as crucial information providers but also in the willingness of clients to pay significant fees for these services. Moreover, both diviners and clients are aware that divination may produce inaccurate results and considerable efforts are made to ensure the accuracy of divinatory verdicts. Here, I summarize empirical evidence focusing on two aspects: the use of repetition to enhance the reliability of information and the strategies employed to distinguish competent diviners from potential quacks and charlatans.

In many ethnographic and historical records, we observe that divinatory procedures are repeated until a consistent verdict appears. In a paradoxical sense, such repetition "ensures" that the revealed information isn't merely due to chance.[19] For example, in both ancient China and ancient Greece, military generals would perform divination procedures multiple times before making important battlefield decisions. As Raphals (2013) notes:

> [There] is evidence in both traditions of ongoing efforts by military leaders to reaffirm divine mandates for military activity. If the primary function of divination were to ensure consensus or military morale, there would be every incentive not to repeat divinatory procedures, at least once a desired response had been obtained. This is exactly the opposite of what we see in Greek military practice. Armies repeatedly performed *hiera*[20] and *sphagia* sacrifices. Similarly in China, even when a military decision had been made at the state level, battlefield divination was repeated continually to determine personnel, to choose auspicious times, and to prognosticate immediate pro-spects for victory.

If we interpret the generals' actions as merely performative or strategic, such repetition would appear puzzling. However, these actions become immediately sensible if we recognize that some generals genuinely wished to follow divine instructions given the great uncertainty and high stakes involved in war. In less serious situations, we similarly observe the tendency to repeat. Among the Nupe people in Nigeria, for instance, diviners in commercial settings might repeat the

---

[19] The modern concept of "chance" associated with probabilistic thinking, however, is shown to be largely absent in pre-modern societies (Berglund, 1976; Hacking, 1990; Hong, 2024; Price, 1975).

[20] Both *hiera* and *sphagia* were sacrificial techniques to reveal divine will in ancient Greece; *hiera* refers to divination through the examination of sacrificial objects (e.g., the liver of a sacrificed sheep), and *sphagia* refers to prayers of supplication or propitiation performed immediately before battle.

casting of shells – similar to the Yoruba's Ifa divination – multiple times, rationalizing that "when you are told something important once only, do you believe it? No – you would wish to hear it twice or three times before you are satisfied that it is the truth. Similarly, you must consult the cords several times." (Nadel, 1954).[21] My own fieldwork among the Nuosu people in southwest China similarly shows that diviners, when using twig divination to generate a yes/no answer, would repeat the same procedure at least twice to confirm the validity of the verdict (Hong & Henrich, 2024). In Taiwanese *Poe* divination, divinatory confirmation typically requires three consecutive positive responses from *poe* throws (statistically similar to coin flipping), and people are aware that the outcomes of these throws are subject to influences other than godly ones (Homola, 2016; Jordan, 1982). The Quiché Mayan requires the same divinatory procedure to be repeated four times with the same result in determining the causes of illness (Bunzel, 1952). Perhaps the most striking example of the measures taken to ensure the accuracy of divinatory verdicts is the Azande chicken oracle, as documented by Evans-Pritchard (1937). The Azande pose a question to the oracle and feed fowls (chickens) with poison, observing whether the fowl dies or survives to determine the verdict. Notably, multiple tests were often conducted to confirm the verdict. Evans-Pritchard (1937) provides a concrete example:

> *First Test.* If X has committed adultery poison oracle kill the fowl. If X is innocent poison oracle spare the fowl. The fowl dies.
>
> *Second Test.* The poison oracle has declared X guilty of adultery by slaying the fowl. If its declaration is true let it spare this second fowl. The fowl survives.
>
> *Result.* A valid verdict. X is guilty.

This example illustrates the logic of Zande divination: By posing the question in the opposite ways, they confirm the consistency and reliability of the outcome generated by the divinatory procedure. The ingenuity of this setup is that it eliminates the possibility of the poison being too strong or too weak in which case the fate of the fowl would be determined by the physical-chemical properties of the poison itself rather than the oracle which supposedly answers the question through controlling the fate of the fowl.[22]

---

[21] Nadel offers an alternative explanation here, suggesting that the diviner may merely try to obtain an arrangement that he could more readily interpret. But the fact that diviner justifies his action in cognitive terms means that he expects his clients to find the truth-reassuring aspect convincing.

[22] A similar kind of technique to check the reliability of individual divinatory setups is to "test" them with self-evident questions. In Mambila spider divination, for example, diviners ask either "Am I here?" or "Will I eat *fufu* (maize porridge) today?" to confirm that the spider is telling the truth. If a spider fails these tests, it is discarded as being unreliable and not fit for use in divination (Zeitlyn, 2012).

In addition to the doubts regarding the reliability of individual divinatory instances, people often hold critical attitudes towards individual diviners. They are acutely aware of the possibility that the works of diviners may be deceptive or fraudulent (Sawden, 2018), and sometimes would frankly acknowledge that many diviners are liars (Evans-Pritchard, 1937; Faki et al., 2010; Mbiti, 1969). This skepticism drives diviners to demonstrate their expertise by commenting on the client's past and present situations – remarks that, though merely confirming what the client already knows or can easily verify, serve as "retrodictions" to showcase their supposed insight (Homola, 2016). Clients might even test a diviner's abilities by asking questions to which only they know the answer or by withholding information, a strategy aimed at validating the diviner's responses (Homola, 2016; van Beek, 2015). Heald (1991) documents a case among the Gisu people where a schoolboy suffering from an illness went to a diviner who attempted to elicit information by running through one potential causative agent after another with the associated symptoms:

> First, he opined that the illness had been sent by the ancestral powers, a judgement he supported by referring to the writing on the page and again by opening the Koran. Charles [the client] and his brother made no response. Moving on, he suggested that it was the ancestral ghosts and asked Charles if he ever dreamt of the ghosts. That would disturb his mind and prevent him from concentrating on his studies. Charles denied it and went on to deny the next suggestion that maybe his joints sometimes felt weak-again, symptomatic of an attack by the ghosts. Well then, Juma [the diviner] hazarded, perhaps he had been bewitched? In that event, the book indicated, it would be someone related to him as 'mother', and at this point he ran through a number of common Gisu women's names. Charles refused them all . . . the session was evidently not felt to have been a success.

What's perhaps more telling is that the client later admitted that he himself suspected that his illness was likely due to witchcraft, and that one of the names that the diviner suggested had indeed been possible. However, he was not going to tell Juma; he wanted Juma to tell him. In Heald's (1991) words, "the diagnosis had to meet the acid test of plausibility, usually by confirming suspicions already entertained by the enquirer."

The skepticism toward individual diviners is evident from the common practice of consulting multiple diviners, a practice that is customary and sometimes even recommended. In many African traditions, many clients would "shop around" for suitable diviners (Fernandez, 1967). Among the Nuosu in southwest China, for example, divination has become a commercial activity in marketplaces, where it is not uncommon for people to seek advice from several diviners (Hong & Henrich, 2024). This is especially true in medical contexts where patients and their families are eager to restore health. Ample ethnographic records have shown that a second opinion may be sought for additional confirmation (Bunzel, 1952; Gelfand, 1956; Mendonsa, 1976; van Beek, 2015), or when one diviner's diagnosis and proposed treatment (usually involving sacrifice to appease the ghosts/spirit) fails (Berglund, 1976; Wilson, 1959). In fact, many medical anthropologists have long pointed out the similarity between divinatory and medical diagnosis (Bunzel, 1952; Fortes, 1966).

Another type of situation where more than one diviner is needed is where potential social conflict is involved and there is pressure for the verdict to appear objective, such as witchcraft and sorcery accusations (Holleman, 1969; Junod, 1927; Turnbull, 1965). Holleman (1969) gives a generic description of such practice among the Shona people in Zimbabwe:

> A woman may by divination be 'proved' guilty of having caused illness or death. In such cases the head of the vakuwasha may require every woman in his village to produce something belonging to them as a token (e.g., a piece of cloth or a string of beads). These makumwa (from kukumba, to collect) are then sent to a diviner, who will retain all tokens except the one belonging to the woman he finds to be guilty. When this token is returned to the village the women are called together again and asked to identify it. The woman who recognizes the token as her own, knows that she is labelled as a muroyi and that she cannot expect to stay in the village. She may sometimes query the verdict and demand that another diviner be consulted. She may then either be exonerated or found guilty again. If guilty, her husband will send her back to her family and demand a dissolution of the marriage.

Witchcraft accusations carry serious consequences, making it crucial for those involved to be cautious about the final verdict. To avoid potential conflicts of interest, it is not uncommon for an "outside" diviner to be consulted (Turnbull, 1965, p. 75). More generally, familiarity between the diviners and clients is often seen as problematic because it makes it difficult to distinguish a "genuinely capable" diviner from a quack who appears to offer accurate predictions simply because they know their clients better (also a form of "ostensive detachment"). In eastern and southern Africa, diviners seldom know their clients because "foreign" diviners are intentionally sought to ensure objectivity (Colson, 1966). For instance, among the Chagga-Rombo people of Kilimanjaro, clients prefer diviners living in villages other than their own, and people may travel considerable distances to see someone in particular (Myhre, 2006). Similarly, the Gisu people in Uganda tend to consult distant diviners who do not know about their cases via local gossip (Heald, 1991). These practices highlight the emphasis on the accuracy and objectivity of divination as an information-generating activity.

4.2 The Primacy of Cognition in Understanding Divination

Human actions usually have some foundation in cognition (Comaroff & Comaroff, 2018). While it is often difficult to distinguish genuine belief from political or social expediency based on manifested action in historical and ethnographic studies (Hankinson, 1988), to deny the cognitive aspect is to treat people engaging in these actions as mindless zombies, which is not only factually incorrect but in a paradoxical sense disrespectful.[23] On the other hand, emphasizing the role cognition plays in divination – and religious actions in general – does not negate the symbolic or functional effects of these practices, but rather highlights that it is inappropriate to completely ignore the cognitive aspects of the actors involved. As Driediger-Murphy (2019) comments on much contemporary theorization on religious sacrifice in ancient Rome:

> In this currently dominant vision of Roman sacrifice, the emphasis is on the social and political functions that sacrifice fulfilled by reminding all involved in it (Gods, humans of various levels of status, animals) of their place in Roman society. Now, it is undoubtedly true that sacrifice did fulfil these functions. But once again, the question that is seldom asked is whether this is what it was about sacrifice that mattered to Romans. My point is not that one explanation is 'wrong' and the other 'right', but simply that if we focus too much on our own functionalist and pragmatic explanations of what sacrifice was doing, we run the risk of missing what it was that its practitioners found interesting, important, challenging, or inspiring about it.

Indeed, functional accounts often omit the actors' emic understanding of their own cultural practices, sometimes to the point of treating such understanding as irrelevant. I would make a further point that functional explanations make sense only in light of the actors' belief in the efficacy of these practices. This is because the functional consequences of technological practices crucially depend on people's belief in these practices fulfilling their instrumental goals. In the case of divination, this means that their social and political functions depend on people placing some faith in divination's epistemic value.

For example, there is ample evidence for the use of divination in military settings in ancient Greece (Anderson, 1970). While one could argue that the generals manipulated omens strategically, such as to launch the attack at the optimal timing (Burn, 1962; Hignett, 1963), the utility of such manipulation depends on the soldiers' belief that reading the body of sacrificial animals is a sensible way of receiving divine messages (the reader could imagine how the soldiers in a secular,

---

[23] Compare Sørensen's (2007) comment on the symbolist interpretation of magic: "In trying to save 'primitive man' from being wrong, that is, basing some of his technology on magic, the symbolist ends up making a much graver allegation, namely that 'primitive man' does not even know why he is doing what he does, but needs the observer to tell him."

modern army would react if a military commander did this). A more dramatic example is the use of inauspicious astronomical phenomena for political purposes in early China. In the Chinese tradition, *yinghuoshouxin* (Mars at Antares) refers to the astronomical phenomenon where the planet Mars appears to be very close to the star Antares in the constellation Scorpius and was considered an extremely inauspicious sign for rulers, who sometimes would push the responsibility to his ministers (Sun & Kistemaker, 1997). Zhang & Huang (1990) analyzed a detailed case where a "Mars at Antares" sign was fabricated in the year 7 BCE (modern astronomical calculations show this phenomenon was impossible that year) during the Han dynasty, and the chancellor was forced by the emperor to commit suicide to claim responsibility. Again, the effectiveness of such manipulation lies in the audience's recognition of the validity of information generated by divination. Elvin (1998) makes this point more explicitly when describing how Yongzheng Emperor of the Qing dynasty interpreted an unusual natural sign – the unusually clear flow of the usually muddy Yellow River – to enhance his political legitimacy:[24]

> The Yongzheng Emperor, still haunted by the accusation that he was a usurper, was seizing on this unusual behavior by the Yellow River to prove his legitimacy by maintaining that his late father, the Kangxi Emperor, was showing his approval from the other world. We are back with opportunism, but as I have said already, Yongzheng must have believed that many people would be persuaded by this tortuous nonsense. Without an audience who can be convinced, there is no sense in making such pronouncements. Indeed, there is a risk of mockery.

We may never know the emperor's personal stance on the validity of such signs; indeed, Elvin (1998) comments that Yongzheng's own real thought on this matter remains "a mystery." But what matters for us is the belief of the common people whom the emperor was trying to impress.[25] Ultimately, we need a theory to explain why a significant portion of the population believed in the connection between the signs and the emperors' reign.

---

[24] The emperor's own comment was as follows: "Now, once Heaven has produced [rain-]water, the energy-vitality of Heaven and Earth flows through it. The Yellow River is moreover designated the ancestor of the four great rivers, and corresponds to the Milky Way above. For its clear and peaceful flow to constitute an auspicious portent, a cooperative reaction to the harmony of Heaven must come from somewhere. The Scripture of Songs says: 'King Wen ascends and descends [in Heaven], assisting at the left and the right hand of God:' What this says is that Kin Wen and Heaven shared the same virtue, and that his sons and grandsons received good fortune from him. Our Late Imperial Father has accompanied the magical efficacy of Heaven in being manifest on high. His affectionate concern and guidance are deep and substantial. We have received this auspicious omen with awe." (Elvin, 1998)

[25] Of course, it is theoretically possible that the everybody was skeptical but thought others believed in it in a situation of pluralistic ignorance (Miller & McFarland, 1987). This, however, was highly unlikely, given the pervasiveness of the supernatural worldview in many traditional societies (Sahlins, 2022).

4.3 The Psychological Basis of Divination

Recall our definition of divination as implausible forms of information technology – given that people seriously intend to employ divination to obtain accurate information, what sustains their belief in these practices if they do not achieve their professed aims? In this section, from a psychological perspective, I discuss both the content-specific factors and general cognitive and cultural-transmission biases that contribute to the belief in the efficacy of divination practices.

Beliefs come in degrees (Frankish, 2009; Moss, 2018). Probabilistically speaking, our belief in the efficacy of some technology may be viewed as a real number between 0 and 1, where 0 represents the belief that the technology will never work and 1 represents the belief that it will always work. In the most general form, such beliefs may be viewed as having an "intrinsic plausibility" component and an "objective reality" component (Figure 2, adapted from Hong and Henrich, 2021). Intrinsic plausibility refers to the extent that the mechanism via which the technology is supposed to work fits our larger, background worldview regarding the causal structures of the universe. Importantly, this includes both evolved intuitions and culturally transmitted worldviews – a point we will return to later in the discussion. The implication here is that "intrinsic plausibility" may vary significantly among people with different worldviews. An individual growing up in a society with a polytheistic belief system, where ghosts and spirits are believed to exist and affect the living in concrete ways, will likely find consulting the divine (narrow-sense divination) quite sensible. In contrast, someone growing up in a scientific culture that denies the existence of supernatural entities may find such practices suspicious. The "objective reality" component, on the other hand, refers to the objective (etic) proportion of the time that the desired outcome is produced when the technology is employed. Crucially, this component takes into account the role of "chance"; for example, a divinatory method that randomly predicts the sex of the fetus will still have a roughly 50 percent success rate. Of course, humans cannot directly perceive objective reality and are subject to various cognitive and transmission biases (Nickerson, 1998; Skowronski & Carlston, 1987; Stahlberg & Maass, 1997).

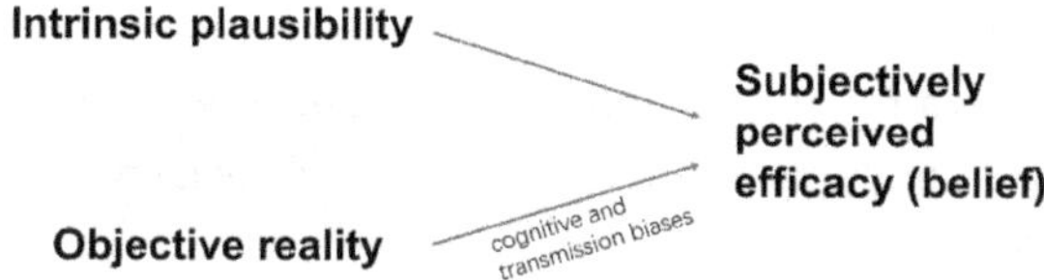

Figure 2 The composition of subjective perception of efficacy (belief).

This account of belief composition has two advantages. First, it clearly acknowledges that people's belief in divination – indeed any technological practices in general – is a function of a multitude of factors, and the breaking down of these factors into two larger categories provides greater analytical clarity on the sources of belief-constituting information and their psychological basis. Second, it allows for a more nuanced understanding of how different individuals and cultures may perceive and evaluate the efficacy of the same practice differently, depending on the idiosyncratic or cultural-specific factors that affect the perception of intrinsic plausibility and objective reality. In the rest of the section I will focus on the intrinsic plausibility aspect of divination and leave the cognitive and transmission biases that distort our perceptions of reality in Section 5.

4.3.1 God(s) as Information Sender: Anthropomorphism and Communication

Let us start with the intrinsic plausibility component of divination that has been under much cognitive theorizing (Chalupa, 2014; Mercier & Boyer, 2021; Sørensen, 2021). These accounts argue that specific features of the human mind make certain cultural practices attractive or plausible, often from an evolutionary perspective. In this section, I will focus on one feature that is particularly relevant for narrow-sense divination where some deities are believed to actively send messages to humans: anthropomorphism.

In its broadest sense, anthropomorphism refers to the act of attributing human characteristics (e.g., intentions, motivations, desires, emotions, etc.) to nonhuman animals or objects (Guthrie, 2013), and much has been said about the causes and consequences of anthropomorphic thinking. Guthrie (1980) argues that because the most important aspect of the human social environment is other humans, it makes adaptive sense to over-detect nonhuman objects as human-like. Subsequently, the term "HADD" (hyperactive agency detection device) has been coined to describe the cognitive process in which human attributes are assigned to nonhumans (Barrett, 2000; Ma-Kellams, 2015).[26] Recent advances in the cognitive science of religion have added a nuanced perspective to this discussion. Scholars argue that anthropomorphic ideas gain traction not because humans are "particularly prone" to attributing mental states to objects but because such ideas are counterintuitive in a technical sense: They violate early-developed tacit assumptions about the physical and social world, such as object

---

[26] Note that this view has been challenged by some evolutionary theorists; see Planer & Sterelny (2022). For a more up-to-date review of the relevant cognitive biases underlying supernatural beliefs, see Willard et al. (2023).

permanence or the boundaries between living and nonliving entities (Boyer, 1996). This violation of intuitive expectations makes anthropomorphic notions attention-grabbing and therefore better suited for cultural transmission. On the other hand, there are also situational factors that may encourage anthropomorphic thinking such as loneliness or when other explanatory systems fail us (Waytz et al., 2010a, 2010b).

Many religious, magical, and superstitious beliefs have been explained through anthropomorphic terms, and the prevalence of anthropomorphic thinking in human societies means that many cultural practices involving human–divine interaction can be easily understood using the same logic that applies to human–human interaction (Horton, 1960). For example, in many traditional societies Gods and deities may be not only pleaded with, but also manipulated, bribed, or even coerced (Cohen, 1978; Hong et al., 2024), just like humans.

One of the most important human activities is intentional communication (Heintz & Scott-Phillips, 2023), and we by default assume that communicated information is relevant to matters at hand (Wilson & Sperber, 2012) and true (Bergstrom et al., 2006; Gilbert et al., 1993). In other words, we live in an environment where we constantly send and receive information intentionally and frequently rely on such information for making decisions. In this communicative aspect, therefore, anthropomorphism manifests itself as positing and acting upon the existence of knowledgeable agents (e.g., the divine) capable of revealing important information – hence, narrow-sense divination. This is most clearly seen in the case of spirit possession where the divination specialists serve as the medium for divine messages (Cohen, 2007) and ancient Greek oracles where enquirers directly pose their questions to priests/priestesses who provide answers on behalf of Gods (Scott, 2014), but is generally applicable to a wide range of information-seeking activities (not necessarily divination); a very recent example may be the anthropomorphizing of artificial intelligence, in particular, robots (Yogeeswaran et al., 2016) and large language models (Wester et al., 2023).

Recognizing the role of anthropomorphism, in particular the projection of human psychological properties onto the divine in narrow-sense divination help explain a number of its features. For example, when information is intentionally sought, some form of "payment" is often required. Note that this is different from payment made to the diviner – the "intermediary" between the divine and the client so to speak– but rather offerings to the divinity itself in exchange for information. Such offerings could be in the form of sacrifice, with extispicy (divination by inspecting the sacrificed animals) being the prime example where the divine message is revealed inside the body of the sacrificial animal (Furley & Gysembergh, 2015), or something more symbolic such as libations (pouring liquids like wine or oil as offerings to deities) (Gaifman, 2018). Sometimes, efforts are made to ensure that the deities receive the enquirers' questions. In traditional Chinese folk religions, for example, incenses are frequently burnt at the start of divinatory rituals with the belief that as the smoke curls up to the heavens where deities live, they will be attracted to its fragrant smell and shift their attention towards offerings and petitions (Habkirk & Chang, 2017; Huang, 2022).

4.3.2 The World as an Interconnected Whole: Holistic Worldviews and Promiscuous Causal Learning

In a way, anthropomorphic thinking is important for narrow-sense divination by definition. What about divination practices that do not presume anthropomorphized entities? As Boyer (2020) points out, divination (by which he means broad-sense divination in the topology that I propose) works fine without hidden agents. This is particularly true in many modern forms of divination such as palm reading and tarot cards as well as ancient numerological practices with strong computational components such as the *Yijing*. Sørensen (2021) argues that in cases where the signs are not understood as communicative, it is our ordinary cognitive apparatus that identifies cause–effect relationships (e.g., intuitive causal reasoning, associative learning, cultural learning, etc.) that serve as the cognitive basis of these practices. Some of these cause–effect relationships have a stronger intuitive component; Sørensen (2021) discusses how intuitive physics, the innate expectations about the causal properties of objects could lead to predictions about the causal unfolding of events, but more generally it could refer to any causal associations[27] that we find plausible in the absence of empirical data. Dreams, for example, are almost universally deemed as prophetic because of our strong intuition that the vivid experiences that occur during sleep cannot possibly be completely meaningless (D'Andrade, 1961; Nordin, 2023). Other cause–effect relationships depend more on learning, either through individual experiences or cultural contexts. Nonetheless, at a fundamental level, the mind employs the same cognitive mechanism that links ordinary entities and events – such as fire and smoke – to lend plausibility to divination practices that do not involve agents. Indeed, some divinatory techniques have been suggested to have a strong proto-scientific flavor (Richardson, 2010).

All of these cognitive mechanisms broadly apply to human technological practices, and in this section I will focus on a culturally mediated psychological

---

[27] Here, "causal" is to be understood broadly that contains "correlation," as correlation almost always implies unresolved causal structure (Shipley, 2016).

factor that more specifically applies to divination as "implausible information technology": the holistic worldview.[28] From a psychological perspective, holistic worldview refers to the belief that all parts of the universe are intimately interconnected and every part may causally affect (and therefore serve as signs for) one another (Hong, 2024). Ample ethnographic records suggest such holistic worldviews are prevalent in traditional, small-scale societies. In describing Bemba cosmology in the context of African religious traditions, Maxwell (1983) explicitly comments on the holistic aspect of their cosmology:

> Bemba religion is "cosmically holistic." Bemba religion conforms to what Africanists are nearly unanimous in affirming of African religions in general: the universe is conceived variously as a "seamless web of relationships" (Booth, 1978, p. 90) "a rapport of forces" (Tempels, 1945, p. 68), "an organization of diverse relationships ... as a whole" (Parsons, 1964, p. 176), an "immanent occult vitality" (Obiechina, 1975, p. 38), the "fundamental unity ... of reality as a whole" (Theuws, 1964, p. 15) and a "comprehensive whole." (Nürnberger, 1975, p. 174)

The emphasis on cosmic interconnectedness and unity provides the ultimate theoretical justification for the possibility of detecting sign–outcome relationships, which acts as a significant cultural driver for broad-sense divination, particularly when it combines with deterministic thinking[29] (Hong, 2024). Such holistic understandings of the world are ubiquitous and widely documented in historical societies such as China (Wang, 1999), India (Bhawuk, 2010), indigenous America (Peat, 1994), ancient Mesopotamia (Van Binsbergen & Wiggermann, 2000), Greece (Sharples, 1983), and Egypt (Malkowski, 2007), as well as many other contemporary, small-scale societies. Sometimes its relevance to divination is explicitly articulated, as seen in an ancient Babylonian diviner's manual that attempts to theorize the Heaven–earth correspondence: "The signs on earth just as those in the sky give us signals. Sky and earth both produce portents though appearing separately. They are not separate (because) sky and earth are related. A sign that portends evil in the sky is (also) evil in the earth, one that portends evil on earth is evil in the sky" (Oppenheim, 1974).

---

[28] It is important to clarify that I do not treat worldviews – whether holistic or otherwise – as uncaused prime movers. On the contrary, I recognize that complex historical and ecological factors influence how people understand the world at both explicit and implicit levels. However, I believe the question of why people hold particular worldviews is a related but distinct issue that warrants its own focused investigation.

[29] See Price's (1975) description of the Saramaka in French Guiana: "Saramaka cosmology is grounded in the belief that every event has a determinate cause which is, potentially at least, discoverable through divination ... there is a relentless insistence on determinacy, what might seem almost like an obsession with causality."

Similarly, the classic Chinese divination method, the *Yijing,* presupposes that the universe is an organic whole in which Heaven, earth, and humanity are intimately connected (Cheng, 2011). Zhu Xi (1130–1200 CE), a renowned Confucian scholar of the Song dynasty, encapsulates this in his famous commentary on the Yijing:

> The *Book of Changes* (*Yijing*) contains the *Taiji*, which generates the two forms. The *Taiji* is the *Dao*; the two forms are *Yin* and *Yang*. *Yin* and *Yang* are one and the same as the *Dao*. The *Taiji* is the Limitless. In the generation of all things, they carry *Yin* and embrace *Yang*, none lack the *Taiji*, none lack the two forms. The weaving and blending of energies produce endless transformations. (Zhu, 1987)

Here, *Taiji,* often translated as the "supreme ultimate," refers to the cosmological state of the universe, encompassing all levels, while *Yin* and *Yang* represent the complementary forces pervading all existence (Zhang, 2002). Despite the complex language, the message is clear: All things share the same origin and are in a state of constant change and transformation. A notable expression of this philosophical concept is the Heaven–man interaction theory proposed by Dong Zhongshu during the Han dynasty: "The interaction between Heaven and Man is profoundly awe-inspiring. When a nation is about to lose its way and face defeat, Heaven first sends disasters as a warning. If there is no introspection, it then sends strange and ominous signs as an alarm. If still there is no change, damage and defeat will inevitably follow" (Ban, 2022).

In this context, Heaven is portrayed as an anthropomorphic entity sending signals to humans, especially rulers. Although there is some debate regarding the nature of Heaven in traditional Chinese thought (Tseng, 2011), the central concept remains that earthly events are connected to the behavior of rulers through the fundamental unity between Heaven and man,[30] as Dong articulates in his seminal work *the Luxuriant Dew of the Spring and Autumn Annals*: "Heaven is the ancestor of all things; without Heaven, nothing can come into being" (Han, 2015). Likewise, in Western traditions, the principles of cosmic sympathy have often been used to justify the plausibility of sign–outcome relationships that may strike modern observers as odd[31] (Hankinson, 1988; Rapisarda, 2022).

---

[30] The political significance of natural signs (in particular disasters) is also seen in the West; see Rohr (2022).

[31] While cosmic holism often co-exists with belief in divine presence (Jeffers, 2007), this is not necessary. In modern astrology which often self-claims as a science (Heindel, 2006), for example, heavenly bodies are believed to exert influences on earthly objects in purely mechanistic ways (Allum, 2011).

One key consequence of a holistic worldview is that it greatly expands the possibility space of causal relationships and sign–outcome correspondences. Psychologically, this means that people with holistic worldviews are more prone to entertain possible causal links even if these links contradict their preexisting beliefs about the world's causal structures, and are less likely to dismiss co-occurrences as mere chance. I have previously termed such psychological tendency "promiscuous causal attribution," characterized by a lack of principles that could definitively deny certain causal possibilities (Hong, 2023). Consequently, the reason that certain information-generating technologies strike modern observers as implausible – and thus divinatory by the etic definition – is that their presumed mechanisms by which signs and outcomes are connected violate our mechanistic worldview that denies such possibilities[32] (Hong & Henrich, 2021).

4.3.3 Miscellaneous Features That Enhance the Credibility of Divination

Having discussed anthropomorphism and holistic worldview that broadly sustains narrow-sense and broad-sense divination respectively, I will now focus on additional features that enhance the intrinsic plausibility of divination primarily by triggering inference on the reliability of divinatory information. The term "miscellaneous" in the section title does not mean they are unimportant; rather it highlights that there is a diverse range of factors that contribute to the perceived reliability of information generated by divination. Many of these factors are not specific to divination but are more broadly applicable to technological practices in general. In the rest of the section I briefly outline a few main factors that have attracted some attention in the literature: the authority of divination technique, the specialness of divinatory specialists, the design of divination methods that reduces potential suspicion, and the lack of falsifiability in divinatory predictions. Most of these factors relate to a fundamental aspect of human communication – ensuring that the information provider is both competent and benevolent (Sperber et al., 2010). While we can never be fully certain of the accuracy of the information we receive, any feature that can trigger inferences about competence or

---

[32] While many sign-outcome correspondences are factually incorrect by modern scientific standards, the underlying idea of a connected world is in fact quite reasonable. Nothing in our immediate environment exist in isolation and objects are often in complex relationships with one another, and seemingly unrelated events can be causally related. The famous "butterfly effect," which is often used to illustrate the idea that small variances in the initial conditions of some complex system could have profound and widely divergent effects on the systems' outcomes, rests on the notion that the world is deeply interconnected (Vernon, 2017). At a more fundamental level, Newton's law of universal gravitation in modern physics states that any two objects are constantly exerting forces upon each other, and this interconnectedness is a basic aspect of the universe.

benevolence will likely have a selective advantage in a competitive market of divinatory practices and practitioners.

One key factor contributing to the perceived reliability of divinatory information is the source authority of the divination techniques themselves. Typically, the source of divinatory knowledge – often deemed divine or supernatural – is not questioned. In narrow-sense divination, deities are believed to possess far greater wisdom and foresight than humans (Bascom, 1941); in broad-sense divination, the commitment to holistic cosmos means that there necessarily exist many sign–outcome correspondences. However, the finite nature of human cognitive capability means that there is no guarantee that divine messages are faithfully transmitted and signs correctly interpreted. Thus, significant emphasis is placed on the authoritativeness of the technique used.

In traditional societies, such authority often manifests as having a somewhat mysterious origin that traces back to ancient sages or superhuman entities. For instance, the Yijing in Chinese culture owes much of its popularity to its reputed origins in the second millennium BCE (Li, 2018). Similarly, the Ifa divination among the Yoruba is attributed to the mythical supreme creator Qrunmila (Clarke, 1939). In large-scale, modern societies, in contrast, scientific institutions have become the paramount authorities on knowledge, leading to the intriguing phenomenon where some divination methods package themselves as "scientific" and diviners describe their own craft as "science" (Jules-Rosette, 1978). Some popular forms of divination in the broad sense, for instance, have sought to acquire an appearance of scientific legitimacy by packaging themselves as "prediction technologies" (Li, 2018; Matthews, 2017), or by aligning with modern physics through the proposal of a "single unifying principle" that connects disparate phenomena to justify a holistic worldview (Semetsky, 2011).

Yet such authority alone is often not enough. I have previously mentioned that clients are often aware of the existence of charlatans, in particular quack diviners that would tell outright lies for material gain (Mendonsa, 1976). Extensive research in cognitive science indicates that we have evolved psychological defense mechanisms that help us ward off potential misinformation (Clément, 2010; Sperber et al., 2010). Given the epistemic concerns regarding the possibility of deception, the design of divination methods often creates an impression of "objectivity" in the sense that the outcomes of divination are not affected by diviners' personal interests. Ahern (1981) posits that successful divination methods incorporate what she calls a "randomizing device" – an element that ensures, at least in the eyes of the beholders, that no one has inappropriately affected the outcome of the divinatory procedure. Similarly, Boyer (2020) describes a similar feature which he terms "ostensive detachment," wherein the perceived randomness or mechanical nature of the divinatory process signals that the diviner is not involved in the production of the outcomes, particularly in context where people's statements are likely to be partial. More generally, in situations where the diviner has a strategic interest in producing certain outcomes, any cue that contributes to the inferences that the diviner is not actively manipulating the divinatory outcome will enhance the clients' perception of reliability and divination practices with designs signaling objectivity are more likely to be favored.

On the side of diviners, there are also factors that contribute to perceptions of the reliability of information generated, usually though clients' inference about their competence. One such factor is the appearance of diviners. In inspired divination where diviners act as the medium between God(s) and mortals, those with unusual looks or physical abnormalities are often preferred by clients, who view these traits as signs of extraordinary power (Stépanoff, 2015). In technical divination, diviners' age is another salient factor that affects clients' perception of competence. People often prefer older diviners out of the rational motivation that they are more experienced[33] (Hiltunen, 1993). This preference aligns with the broader tendency to trust older individuals in the realm of traditional cultural know-how (Henrich & Broesch, 2011), and the general observation that older people are well-respected and preferentially learned from in small-scale, traditional societies (Maxwell & Silverman, 1970; Simmons, 1945).

I will now turn to the topic of the divinatory outcomes, which are often the primary concern for clients who value their accuracy. It's important to note that divinatory outcomes do not simply "speak for themselves" – even in inspired divination, interpreting the signs typically requires substantial effort (Hong, 2022b). As a result, there is usually ample room for diviners to creatively interpret the meanings of these outcomes (Brown, 2006). Often, diviners have some familiarity with the clients' social background and the type of problems they are likely to encounter, which enables them to provide somewhat accurate analyses of past and present life events related to the matters at hand (Fernandez, 1967, p. 13; Grout, 1864, p. 157; Jules-Rosette, 1978). Yet a more important factor that make divinatory interpretations appear accurate is that they are often sufficiently vague and ambiguous, making falsification difficult. The Delphic oracles in ancient Greece, for example, were notorious for producing ambiguous verdicts such as "a great empire will fall," which was famously ambiguous in its relevance to King Croesus's inquiry about the prospects of invading Persia (Kindt, 2006). A cursory look at the ethnographic records shows that this characteristic is common across various cultures and

---

[33] This stands in contrast with inspired divination where children are sometimes used as spiritual medium due to their perceived innocence and susceptibility to suggestion (Johnston, 2001)

historical periods (Barnett, 1971; Denig & Hewitt, 1930; Ellis, 1917; Grout, 1864). Beattie (1960) describes how Bunyoro diviners in identifying potential sorcerers would "simply say that his shells confirm what the client has himself suggested, or else he indicates the sorcerer in vague terms ('a tall dark man living to the north') which the client himself applies to the person he suspects"; Hallowell (1942) notes that the skill of diviners among the Saulteaux lies primarily in "replying in ambiguous terms upon all subjects of which he has not been able to procure information in advance," ensuring that the diviner is "always sure of success, either more or less striking." Researchers interested in the psychology of superstition have also noted this aspect of divinatory verdicts; in astrology, the vague yet seemingly specific predictions are known as "the Barnum effect" (named after the nineteenth-century showman Phileas Barnum), referring to the phenomenon where people tend to believe a statement about their personality that is vague or trivial if they think that it derives from some systematic procedure tailored especially for them (Dickson & Kelly, 1985; Furnham & Schofield, 1987).

5 Divination in Society – The Interplay of Individual Cognition and Societal Processes

Thus far, I have primarily discussed aspects of divination and the relevant sociocultural variables (e.g., holistic worldviews) that enhance its intrinsic plausibility. However, there's more to the story; the outcomes of divination always matter, and people generally[34] prefer accurate information over inaccuracy (Hong & Henrich, 2021). Moreover, the nature of certain inquiries leads to divinatory verdicts that are not open to interpretation; for instance, fetal sex prognostication typically yields an unambiguous answer that is verifiably right or wrong (Ostler & Sun, 1999). Why, then, do people not realize that these divination methods fail to provide accurate information? Note that from the empirical perspective, failing to provide accurate information means not outperforming chance. This is important because sometimes diviners do deliver correct verdicts "by chance" – in the case of predicting the sex of the fetus, even random guessing would achieve a 50 percent success rate. Throughout this section, I will keep using fetal sex prediction as an example because human sex determination is one of the few cases where the probability of a naturally occurring and culturally significant outcome is scientifically known (Hong & Zinin, 2023), and it gives us a reference point for evaluating the factors that bias

---

[34] In rare cases, people might prefer not knowing the truth for reasons relating to psychological comfort. This is sometimes termed "blissful ignorance" in the literature (Lupton et al., 1991).

our subjective perception of accuracy, particularly how social information can cause it to deviate from objective reality.

5.1 Efficacy Assessment as a Social Process

As an ultra-social species, we rely heavily on socially transmitted information (Boyd et al., 2011). Due to the cumulative nature of human cultural knowledge, many cultural products and technologies cannot be fully understood by individuals alone and necessarily require faith and social signals of their utility (Henrich, 2016). In other words, Individuals' firsthand, personal experiences are often insufficient to form beliefs that guide actions. In divination, this means that in addition to personal experiences, both testimonial[35] (transmitted stories of divination yielding accurate information) and observational (people turning to divination in cases of uncertainty) information is taken into account when we assess the overall efficacy of some divination method.

Let's first consider the influence of testimonials using fetal sex prediction as an example. Imagine an individual experiencing a 50 percent (i.e., chance level) success rate of some fetal sex prediction method through firsthand encounters. The individual may nonetheless encounter stories told by others where 90 percent of divination instances are reported as yielding accurate information as a result of selective reporting. To analyze how these two types of information influence an individual's beliefs, we can apply Bayesian belief updating, a statistical method that updates the probability estimate for a hypothesis as additional evidence is learned. In this context, "priors" refer to the initial beliefs about a parameter or hypothesis before new data are observed, while "posteriors" refer to updated beliefs after new data have been taken into account. From this perspective, integrating firsthand experiences and anecdotal reports will result in a "posterior" belief that lies between 50 and 90 percent, depending on the relative weight assigned to each type of evidence.[36] This is, of course, not to say that humans are fully rational Bayesian updaters; they are emphatically not (Albert, 2009). What matters for our purposes, however, is that the direction of human belief updating should be in line with Bayesian rationality. In other words, we should generally expect individuals' prior belief of 50 percent due to personal experience to increase rather than decline in response to testimonial evidence of a 90 percent success rate. The preferential reporting of divinatory successes, combined with the well-known confirmation bias where individuals selectively remember and recall information that aligns with their prior beliefs

---

[35] Here I'm using "testimony" in a technical way, which is narrower in scope than its common use in social epistemology (Goldman, 1994).

[36] For theoretical models that employ this approach, see (Hong, 2022a; Hong & Henrich, 2021).

(Nickerson, 1998), thus could greatly enhance individuals' subjective belief in divination's efficacy and create an overwhelming impression of the accuracy of these predictive technologies.

But do divinatory successes really get preferentially transmitted? In a series of studies, I and my colleagues have shown that individuals have a strong tendency to report the outcomes of successful magic and divination rituals (Hong, 2022b, 2022c; Hong et al., 2024; Hong & Zinin, 2023), consistent with research in social medicine where favorable and positive outcomes are preferentially reported (De Barra, 2017; De Barra et al., 2014). On the very topic of fetal sex prediction, we performed a systematic examination of documented instances of fetal sex prediction across various genres of historical texts – including oracle bone inscriptions, dynastic histories, encyclopedias, and local gazetteers – and found that the reported predictive success rates are consistently high, around 90 percent (Hong & Zinin, 2023). A naïve reader exposed to these stories that highlight the efficacy of fetal sex prognostication methods is likely to make the false generalization that these methods are effective, at least in theory.

In addition to testimonial information that enhances people's estimates of efficacy, observing others engaging in divinatory activities can also increase efficacy estimates through an inference chain: "other people perform divination when they need information → other people believe in divination's efficacy → divination is efficacious." The first inference is relatively straightforward: Goal-directedness is a basic psychological tendency, and individuals naturally interpret an agent's actions as purposefully directed towards achieving a particular object-ive (Harris, 2006). More generally, humans are predisposed to interpret other people as intentional agents whose actions aim to accomplish specific goals (Dennett, 1987; Mackey, 2016), and the most direct inference from observing people resort to divination is often their belief in its efficacy.

The second inference, however, is less tenable from a strictly philosophical perspective, and adopting beliefs simply because others hold them is often viewed as the antithesis of critical thinking – an Enlightenment ideal that traces back to philosophers like Locke and Descartes (Levy, 2022). Yet, as a practical heuristic for mimicking others, this type of inference generally functions well, especially when the actions observed are costly (Henrich, 2009). In fact, our day-to-day functioning heavily relies on our default trust in others – that they are not intentionally deceiving us. In some cases, actions may even carry more epistemic weight than words in influencing our own decision-making, as reflected in the saying "actions speak louder than words."

We therefore should expect individuals' subjective belief in efficacy to be further boosted as a result of such observational learning. Note that in our stylized example, we haven't considered the epistemic influence of intrinsic plausibility; in reality, certain fetal sex prediction methods may align with people's intuitive understanding of the world (e.g., methods based on yin-yang theory in traditional China) and may additionally enhance individuals' subjective belief. In Hong and Henrich (2021), we formally model the belief updating process within a dynamic population setting where individuals are constantly observing and learning from one another. The main takeaway from the study is that personal experience is just one of many factors affecting individuals' subjective estimates of efficacy. Once social learning is accounted for, it becomes clear how subjective beliefs can be amplified by various types of transmitted information.

5.2 Human Culture as Imposing "Priors" and Evidential Standards for Divination

In the previous section, I discussed how socially transmitted information, when combined with other types of data, contributes to the belief updating process. However, human culture in a broader sense can also directly influence the intrinsic plausibility of various divination methods through culturally transmitted worldviews, or meta-understandings of the causal structures of the world. In Section 4.3.2, I examined how a holistic worldview may facilitate promiscuous causal learning. I now wish to highlight that in most parts of the modern world, this holistic understanding has been largely supplanted by a worldview that actively denies the causal relevance between events that do not have plausible physical connections (Hong & Henrich, 2021). It is important to note that this new worldview does not deny promiscuous causality in the absolute sense; indeed, according to Newton's law of universal gravitation, any two objects are constantly exerting forces upon each other, and such interconnectedness is a fundamental feature of the universe. Rather, it posits that many events and objects are *practically* causally irrelevant, in the sense that the causal impact may be too weak to be observable or meaningful (Hong, 2024). One prominent contemporary critique of astrology, for instance, argues that celestial bodies are too distant to exert any meaningful influence on us (Bok et al., 1975).

The influence of culturally transmitted worldviews on the plausibility of divinatory methods is also clearly manifested in narrow-sense divination. By definition, the validity of narrow-sense divination depends on a background belief in supernatural entities, and is sometimes further legitimized by the recognition of witchcraft and sorcery as realities that humans have to deal with (Faki et al., 2010). Surely, there is no point in consulting the divine if such entities do not exist. Though in many ways anthropomorphic thinking and the resultant religious representations may be considered human beings' cognitive and cultural defaults, with psychologists fond of noting that magico-religious thinking is often present in modern, contemporary humans as it was in the ancients (Nemeroff & Rozin, 2000; Subbotsky, 2010), the reality is that a significant portion of today's population does not believe in ghosts, spirits, or other supernatural entities[37] (Bullivant et al., 2019), and divination has largely disappeared from at least the surface of daily life in modern societies (Burkert, 2005). Our understanding of the world has shifted from a theistic one to a mechanistic one which leaves little room for anthropomorphic deities that communicate with humans (Fourie, 1988).

The profundity of the shift from a holistic, interconnected world where deities interacted with humans to a disconnected, materialistic one where possible superhuman entities are no longer acknowledged and possible causal relationships constrained, cannot be overstated. This transition underpins the intuition behind the etic definition of divination as implausible information technology; as modern observers, certain information-generating methods strike us as implausible because they violate our culturally transmitted assumptions about the ontological structures of the world. Indeed, the decline of divination in many parts of the world must be considered in the context of the diffusion of Western science (Hong & Henrich, 2021). In both China and Japan, for example, the superiority of Western science and technology was quickly recognized during extensive cultural contact with the West in the nineteenth century (Waley, 1958; Hones & Endo, 2006), and many intellectual elites increasingly began to critically assess their own traditions. During the Meiji restoration in Japan, with the establishment of Western style scientific and educational institutions (Bartholomew, 1989), many traditional cultural practices and beliefs were labeled "superstitious," and some were banned at the legislative level (Figal, 1999). In China, divination, along with a range of other traditional cultural practices, came to be viewed as an irrational superstition to be eradicated (Zhiwei, 2009). Progressive scholars in particular attacked the theoretical basis of divination (and superstitions in general) and often made explicit contrast with modern science. Chen Duxiu, a leader of the New Culture Movement in the early twentieth century in China, famously criticized these practices: "If one believes that science is the compass that points to truth, then things that contradict science like ghosts, spirits, alchemy, talismans, fortune telling, divination, spirit writing, feng shui, and the theory of Yin and Yang are all utter nonsense and absolutely not to be trusted" (Chen, 1915).

---

[37] In sociology, much research has been devoted to explaining this phenomenon, and is often referred to as the "secularization thesis" (Pasquale & Kosmin, 2013; Voas & Chaves, 2016).

In addition to blunt attacks, naturalistic explanations were sometimes provided for both why people resort to superstition and the insidious intentions of their practitioners. In a Shenbao article published in 1939, the author made such an argument explicitly:

> Dream divination, fortune-telling, and other such practices are acts of superstition, while deities, Buddhas, ghosts, and spirits are objects of their superstition ... According to modern scientific interpretation, dreams and spirit writing are merely subconscious acts of self-deception. Deities, Buddhas, ghosts, and spirits are at most fabrications by religious figures intended to reclaim the morality of the public, tools used to frighten women, children, and the ignorant.[38]

It's important to note that the shift in worldview was gradual, and for a considerable time, even the literati continued to engage in various superstitious activities (Xiong, 2015). However, as science became the dominant framework to understand the world, divination and other superstitious practices were increasingly marginalized (Li & Lang, 2012). In the Republic of China era, such marginalization was sustained by state-level legislative efforts and educational programs aimed at eradicating superstitions. Materialistically, this was most salient in the destruction of temples or their repurposing into schools or secular public venues, as well as regulations outlawing ritual activities (Zhu, 2013). Although we do not have definitive evidence of the extent to which people's beliefs were affected and much literature on this topic tends to emphasize how folk religious practices *persisted* in such anti-superstition movements (Katz, 2013), it is undeniable that divination, magic, and other superstitious practices have since been relegated to the margins of societies. In the West, such transition occurred much earlier (Thomas, 2003) and these "past irrationalities" were already treated as ancient survivals and documented by folklorists during Victorian times (Walsham, 2008).

The significant cognitive consequence of this worldview change is elegantly summarized by the sociological concept of a "disenchanted world," originally proposed by Max Weber (Greisman, 1976). Here, "disenchantment" refers to the devaluation of religion and the emphasis on rationality, characteristic of modernized, bureaucratic, secularized Western societies, which contrast sharply with traditional societies where "the world remains a great enchanted garden" (Weber, 1922). Although recent scholarship has challenged the Weberian thesis, arguing either that magic has survived disenchantment (Hanegraaff, 2003) or that the world is experiencing a re-enchantment (Landy & Saler, 2009), we can't ignore the brute fact divination and magic have largely lost the cognitive appeal

---

[38] Author name is Shang Qing (尚卿); Shenbao, July 18, 1939; no. 23485.

that they once had for a significant proportion of humanity, as people become increasingly skeptical towards the postulated superhuman entities and the presumed causal mechanisms that magicians and diviners rely upon. A person with a scientific outlook does not need empirical data to be deeply suspicious of the claim that illnesses can be diagnosed by examining the holes thigh bones of a sacrificed chicken (Hong & Henrich, 2021). The very features that once bolstered the plausibility of divinatory practices now often raise red flags in the modern context.

In addition to affecting the intrinsic plausibility of divination through modifying the "priors," a scientific culture also influences how we recognize, collect, and process evidence in subtle yet significant ways. Modern societies feature a distinct division of labor in knowledge production and transmission: scientists as the producers and laypeople as the consumers of knowledge. Scientists systematize personal and anecdotal experiences, transforming personal experiences into randomized, controlled trials and anecdotes into meta-reviews and meta-analyses, and in doing so largely avoid the underreporting of negative evidence and other biases. As a result, for lay people, accepting expert opinion is a far more dependable route to truth since our epistemic environment is structured to be more reliable (Levy, 2022). Additionally, even those not professionally involved in science develop an understanding of reliable knowledge production; for instance, one does not need to be a scientist to know that the evaluation of the efficacy of drugs requires randomized, controlled trials (minimally, some kind of experimentation), or that a neighbor's anecdotal story of her horoscope correctly predicting her personality does not qualify as evidence for the validity of astrology (Hong & Henrich, 2021). More crucially, the very concept of "chance-level performance" often requires a substantial amount of statistical education, and people without such concepts may not even consciously consider whether the perceived efficacy of some divinatory practice exceeds chance. For example, many Nuosu individuals with little education in contemporary southwest China think that a diviner with a 50 percent success record in fetal sex prediction is demonstrating mediocre to good ability, not recognizing that this is merely the expected success rate for random guessing (Hong, 2022c). In contrast, a modern reader with some understanding of statistics would easily recognize that a 50 percent success rate for an outcome with dichotomous, equiprobable options merely matches the expectations of random chance, indicating no actual divining ability. Without such a conceptual benchmark for evaluating efficacy, divination methods that produce correct outcomes at sufficiently high frequency due to natural stochasticity may persist as they appear to "work" from time to time.

It is worth noting that even systems explicitly designed to minimize false positives, such as modern science, can become unreliable when safeguards are weakened. Practices like p-hacking and other questionable research practices (QRPs) – such as selectively reporting results or testing multiple hypotheses without corrections – can inflate the likelihood of statistically significant but unreliable findings (Fiedler & Schwarz, 2016). P-hacking, which involves manipulating data analysis to achieve statistically significant results, often produces findings that appear meaningful but fail to replicate, undermining the credibility of the research (Head et al., 2015). However, the scientific community is acutely aware of these issues and actively works to address them through initiatives such as open science practices (Banks et al., 2019), preregistration of studies (Nosek et al., 2018), and replication efforts (Lindsay, 2015). These measures aim to reduce biases and improve the reliability of scientific findings. Such awareness and commitment to improve integrity and reliability contrast sharply with divinatory practices, where mechanisms for evaluating validity are often absent.

6 Conclusions, Outstanding Questions, and Future Directions

Throughout this Element I have advocated a commonsense approach to understanding divination, emphasizing the instrumental role it plays in daily life and the centrality of cognition in making sense of its functional effects. I wish to emphasize that divination as "implausible information-generating technology" is an unusual definition in scholarly discourse, and I have not focused as much on traditional markers of divination such as ritualistic repetition and randomization (Lisdorf, 2007; Sørensen, 2021). While these features do often enhance the intrinsic plausibility of divination, they are neither necessary nor sufficient conditions and are only intelligible in specific cultural contexts. People's belief in the efficacy of any predictive technology is always subject to a multitude of psychological, social, and cultural factors. Anthropomorphic thinking and holistic worldviews contribute to the plausibility of narrow-sense and broad-sense divination respectively, and selective reporting of divination successes and the inference of divination's efficacy from its observed use in uncertain situations further bolster people's confidence in these practices. I concluded by underscoring the profound yet nuanced impact of human culture in introducing new worldviews, establishing reliable epistemic institutions, and setting evidential standards. These cultural shifts provide the necessary cognitive tools to effectively evaluate different sources of information.

So, have we solved the puzzle of *why divination persists* despite its objective ineffectiveness? I believe we are making significant progress, along the general lines of inquiry into why certain cultural products are successful. However, as is often the case in science, unanswered questions remain. In this final section,

I propose two outstanding questions that may merit further theoretical and empirical investigation, the first applying specifically to divination, while the second applies more generally to human technological practices.

6.1 The Precision versus Accuracy Trade-off in Divination

In Section 4.3.3, I highlighted how the vagueness of divinatory verdicts, such as the Barnum effect in astrology, may enhance people's belief in the efficacy of divinatory practices. The advantage of vague predictions is clear: They evade falsification, allowing clients to affirm their existing trust in the diviner's competence or the divination method's validity. However, ethnographic and historical evidence suggests that clients are often more impressed by precise predictions.

In this context, "precise predictions" refer to what philosopher of science Karl Popper describes as "risky predictions" – specific and bold forecasts that risk being disproven (Popper, 2005). Ethnographic studies highlight a preference among clients for diviners and divination systems that can provide more specific answers (van Beek et al., 1994, p. 221). These diviners sometimes demonstrate impressive accuracy, revealing knowledge of clients' personal experiences that are so private and rare that it is unlikely for a stranger to correctly guess them. In contemporary Chinese divination, clients would often acknowledge that they are impressed by diviners' precision, saying things like " … the diviner said I broke my elbow when I was five years old. I didn't remember that and doubted his words but I was very surprised when my mother later confirmed it" or "the diviner claimed I had a mole on my back. This is amazing, as even my wife had not noticed it" (Li, 2018). As mentioned, these insights typically do not directly facilitate decision-making but rather serve to showcase the diviner's expertise or skill. An extreme example can be seen in Bourdillon's (1976, p. 175) description of a good diviner among the Shona people:

> It is said that a good diviner should know of his prospective clients before their arrival and go out to meet them before they reach his homestead, though in practice this rarely happens. In any case the diviner is supposed to be able to tell the clients what their trouble is before they say anything … The degree of the diviner's foreknowledge, which he is supposed to have received in a dream while his clients were on their way to consult him, affects his prestige.

Conversely, vague predictions can be frowned upon. During fieldwork among the Nuosu in southwest China, I encountered complaints about diviners who make broad, nonspecific predictions that could apply to anyone – such as having red clothes or experiencing headaches – leading to suspicions of deceit (Hong & Henrich, 2024).

The intuition is straightforward. A diviner who offers more specific predictions, such as forecasting a misfortune in January rather than just "next year," when correct, seems more impressive and trustworthy. Yet, precise predictions are inherently riskier and more likely to fail. While many divinatory failures are rationalized away (which relates to the second outstanding question), they nonetheless can diminish confidence in the diviner's skills.

Consequently, a trade-off emerges between precision and accuracy in divination. Diviners aim to showcase their skill by offering precise predictions, yet also strive to enhance their accuracy by crafting predictions that are broad enough to withstand falsification. Ideally, both precision and accuracy are desired, but the nature of divination as an implausible information technology necessitates a compromise. Could there be some optimal balance where accurate predictions are precise enough to impress, yet the number of incorrect predictions doesn't undermine trust excessively?

It is unlikely that there will be a single "sweet spot" across the board, but exploring the trade-off between precision and accuracy in divination may reveal the complex interplay between client expectations and diviner strategies. The preference for precision, while potentially enhancing the reputation of a diviner when predictions are correct, comes with heightened risks of disconfirmation. Vague predictions, on the other hand, minimize the risk of being proven wrong but may not sufficiently impress clients to inspire confidence or repeat consultations.

This dynamic raises several important questions for future research. First, what mechanisms do diviners employ to navigate this trade-off? It would be beneficial to investigate whether diviners consciously adjust the level of precision based on factors such as the perceived skepticism of the client, the seriousness of the inquiry, or their own confidence in the information at hand. Second, how do clients' experiences with both types of predictions influence their long-term beliefs about divination? Understanding this could illuminate the processes through which cultural beliefs about divination are reinforced or challenged over time.

Additionally, the impact of cultural context on this trade-off is profound. In cultures where divination is widely accepted and integrated into the daily life, the balance might lean more towards precision to maintain and enhance the diviner's status, especially given that divinatory failures tend to be under-reported (see Section 5.1). Conversely, in more skeptical environments, the strategy might shift towards safer, more ambiguous predictions to avoid direct challenges and maintain a baseline level of client engagement.

The precision versus accuracy trade-off in divination is not just a theoretical concept but a practical challenge that diviners navigate through every interaction. This ongoing negotiation between diviner and client, shaped by broader cultural and social dynamics, continues to sustain divination as a fascinating subject of study in understanding human cognition, culture, and social interaction. Future research in this area can provide deeper insights into the cognitive underpinnings of belief systems and the complex ways in which humans generate and interpret information about the world.

6.2 Divinatory Failures and the Limit of Post-hoc Rationalization

In the previous section, I briefly touched upon how divinatory failures are often rationalized to protect the core belief in divination's efficacy. Such post-hoc (after the fact) rationalizations are ubiquitous across cultures and historical periods. The key idea is that there are always factors that can be invoked to account for failed predictions without challenging the legitimacy of divination itself. Keith Thomas (2003) famously argued that no amount of failed predictions would shake the faith of true believers because they can always rationalize these failures within their existing belief systems. Evans-Pritchard (1937) documents a similar mode of thinking among the Azande, where individuals were acutely aware of the myriad of factors that could lead to an incorrect verdict in chicken oracle: wrong variety of poison, age of the poison, breach of a taboo, anger of the ghosts, or sorcery (Evans-Pritchard, 1937). Evans-Pritchard refers to the ways in which people try to justify and explain the inconsistencies and contradictions within their belief systems "secondary elaborations," a phenomenon that is prevalent and has been noted by ethnographers (Jordan, 1982). More often, the blame shifts to individual diviners, who are usually considered fallible. The working assumption of the clients is typically that there is, in theory, a correct answer that could be revealed by divination, but that not all diviners are equally skilled to be able to (Bascom, 1941). As a result, clients may suspect individual diviners, but seldom the system as a whole.

In the philosophy of science, these additional factors that account for empirical failures of some theoretical prediction are termed "auxiliary hypotheses" (Hempel, 1966) and have long worried philosophers because they suggest a slippery slope toward unfalsifiability (Harding, 1976). Gershman (2019) recently proposed a Bayesian solution to this conundrum: Observations that appear to contradict a central hypothesis can, under the right circumstances (e.g., if the prior belief in the core theory is sufficiently strong), be "explained away" by changing auxiliary hypotheses in a Bayesian rational manner. In other words, it may be perfectly rational to look for "excuses" instead of abandoning the theory when an unexpected outcome occurs. Consider the discovery of Neptune as an illustration: When anomalies in Uranus's orbit contradicted Newtonian physics, the hypothesis of an unseen planet was posited rather than discarding Newtonian principles, leading to Neptune's discovery in 1846 (Smart, 1946). Indeed, such rationalization is common in contemporary scientific discourse (Blanton et al., 2007) and everyday reasoning (Cushman, 2019; Summers, 2017), ensuring theories are not discarded prematurely.

What does this mean for our understanding of divination? The existence and utility of auxiliary hypotheses in science suggest that employing them to explain inconsistencies in divination isn't inherently irrational. However, Gershman's Bayesian analysis indicates that even when these hypotheses absorb most of the blame, the core theory still suffers epistemically. In other words, if we think our belief in the efficacy of some divinatory method as a value between 0 and 1, auxiliary hypotheses such as the incompetence of the individual diviner or the insincerity of the client can never *fully* protect the core theory that the divination method generates the truth, and our belief in its efficacy should always decrease with each failure, even if only slightly. Over time, this can lead to a cumulative decline in belief. This poses the question: Is there a threshold of disbelief, or must skepticism and change come from outside the belief system itself? Evidence on this topic is mixed. On one hand, numerous observations suggest that faith in divination and religious practices is often insulated from contradictory evidence. Beyond the anecdotal evidence from ethnography, which shows that predictive failures are frequently rationalized, there exists a body of research in sociology and social psychology focused on how religious cults handle failed prophecies. In a seminal study by Festinger et al. (1956), the leader of a cult predicted a catastrophic flood that would destroy much of the United States, with followers to be rescued by aliens. After the prophecy failed, rather than abandoning their beliefs, a small core of the group intensified their proselytizing efforts. Follow-up studies have generally supported these findings, indicating a pattern where beliefs persist despite disconfirming evidence (Dawson, 1999). Some philosophers propose a more radical view, suggesting that religious beliefs function as forms of make-believe that are fundamentally different from factual beliefs and thus impervious to empirical counter-evidence (Van Leeuwen, 2014).

On the other hand, some research suggests that religious adherents often exhibit significant disappointment at failed prophecies, and in some cases, these disillusionments may lead to the disintegration of the group (Stark, 1996). For example, many ethnographers and historians have attributed the decline of the Ghost Dance movement among the Cherokee in the 1800s to unfulfilled predictions, such as a hailstorm that was supposed to destroy the earth and threats of death to nonbelievers, which never materialized (McLoughlin et al., 1984, p. 113). In the Millerite movement in nineteenth-century America, similarly, followers expected the world to end on a specific date based on prophetic calculations. When the world did not end – a day referred to as the "Great Disappointment" – the movement experienced profound turmoil, with many members departing in disillusionment[39] (Knight, 1993). Most divinatory verdicts, of course, are not as dramatic as prophecies, but we'd nonetheless expect them to influence our beliefs in some way. In fact, there are theoretical reasons to expect divinatory failures to carry significant epistemic weight: Researchers in social psychology have identified a "negativity bias," where humans have a propensity to give more weight to negative information than to positive information in contexts such as news selection (Soroka et al., 2019) and impression formation (Skowronski & Carlston, 1989).

The manner in which believers cognitively process counter-evidence has profound implications not only for divination but also for instrumental practices in general. While instrumental religious actions such as rainmaking and fetal sex prognostication occasionally prove successful, what happens in scenarios where failures significantly outnumber successes? Could the cumulative impact of these failures gradually erode faith in the system?[40] Should we expect a cultural evolutionary process in which only those practices and belief systems that effectively withstand counter-evidence survive? Furthermore, if a negative bias is present in divination, how does it reconcile with the selective reporting of positive outcomes, as discussed in Section 5.1? Future research could explore the dynamic interaction between belief change and post-hoc rationalization, in particular, possible thresholds at which repeated divinatory failures begin to outweigh the confirmation and reporting biases that typically maintain such beliefs. Understanding these dynamics could provide deeper insights into how cultural and belief systems evolve or dissolve over time, especially in the face of contradictory evidence.

6.3 Looking Ahead: A Cognitive Theory of Human Technology

Many of the characteristics of divination and features that could enhance people's faith in it in this Element are not exclusive to divination *per se*. In fact, this is necessarily the case given that divination is not qualitatively different from other ordinary information technology in my proposed commonsense, cognitive

---

[39] Though some adherents reinterpreted the prophecy, leading to the formation of the Seventh-day Adventist Church.

[40] One interesting dimension of divination's persistence is the varying rates at which beliefs erode across different domains. For instance, technological advancements such as ultrasound have rendered practices like fetal sex divination largely obsolete by providing a more accurate and reliable alternative. In such cases, people are often willing to adopt the superior information technology because it offers clear predictive advantages. However, even as such practices decline, individuals may continue to attribute some validity to the older methods if there is no shift in their underlying worldview.

framework. Thus, I challenge theories that claim divination possesses a unique rationality (Rapisarda, 2022; Zeitlyn, 2012). All technological practices combine aspects of intrinsic plausibility with elements of objective reality, and in competitive market environments, practitioners must effectively signal their competence to attract clients. What demarcates divination from ordinary information technology – their "supernaturalness" so to speak – is our worldview which no longer acknowledges anthropomorphized deities and a deeply interconnected universe.

The implication is that the theoretical framework and tools that we employ to make sense of ineffective technologies such as divination and magic can also be used to explain the effective ones. For instance, financial analysts and economists are sometimes sarcastically compared to shamans when they fail to accurately predict market movements (Caldararo, 2008; Coggin, 2006). While the original intent of these comparisons may be to highlight the objective ineffectiveness of both financial forecasting and shamanistic divination, the more relevant point for our discussion is their structural similarities as information technologies. Both involve elements of intrinsic plausibility, though these vary significantly depending on the observer's worldview. Unlike divination, which gains plausibility through the assumption of divine influence and a holistic worldview of an interconnected universe, financial analysts in contemporary societies are trusted largely due to our familiarity with the capitalist economic system and our constant interaction with numbers and probabilities. Financial forecasting is further legitimized by endorsements from academic and research institutions, similar to how traditional divination methods draw legitimacy from ancient wisdom. Meanwhile, individual financial analysts, much like diviners, face skepticism when their predictions fail. To explain these failures, analysts might cite limitations in their models, technical issues, or unforeseen market events, mirroring how diviners might attribute their inaccuracies to violations of taboos or sorcery influences.

Can there be a cognitive theory of human technology? I think yes, and I envision such a unified theory would not only elucidate not only the structural parallels between divination and modern technologies like financial or weather forecasting but also offer insights into the cognitive processes that lend both ancient and contemporary technologies their perceived efficacy. By understanding these cognitive underpinnings, we can better comprehend how certain technologies – whether labeled as divinatory or scientific – maintain their credibility and influence across various cultures and historical contexts.

References

Ahern, E. M. (1981). *Chinese ritual and politics*. Cambridge University Press.

Ajala, A. S. (2013). Ifa divination: A diagnostic and therapeutic device in Yoruba healing system. In P. M. Peek & W. E. A. van Beek (Eds.), *Reviewing reality: Dynamics of African divination* (pp. 115–138). LIT Verlag.

Albert, M. (2009). Why Bayesian rationality is empty, perfect rationality doesn't exist, ecological rationality is too simple, and critical rationality does the job. *Rationality, Markets and Morals, 0*(3). https://ideas.repec.org/a/rmm/journl/v0y2009i3.html.

Allum, N. (2011). What makes some people think astrology is scientific? *Science Communication, 33*(3), 341–366.

Anderson, J. K. (1970). *Military theory and practice in the age of Xenophon*. University of California Press.

Annus, A. (2010). On the beginnings and continuities of omen sciences in the ancient world. In A. Annus (Ed.), *Divination and the interpretation of signs in the ancient world* (pp. 1–18). Oriental Institute of the University of Chicago.

Ban, G. (2022). Hanshu 漢書. In 點校本二十四史：大字本 *[Annotated and Collated Edition of the Twenty-Four Histories]*. Zhonghua shuju.

Banks, G. C., Field, J. G., Oswald, F. L. et al. (2019). Answers to 18 questions about open science practices. *Journal of Business and Psychology, 34*, 257–270.

Baratz, A. (2022). The roots of divination in archaic poetry. *Classical Philology, 117*(4), 581–602.

Barnard, A. (2021). *History and theory in anthropology*. Cambridge University Press.

Barnett, W. K. (1971). *An ethnographic description of Sanlei Ts'un, Taiwan, with emphasis on women's roles overcoming research problems caused by the presence of a great tradition*. University Microfilms.

Barrett, J. L. (2000). Exploring the natural foundations of religion. *Trends in Cognitive Sciences, 4*(1), 29–34. https://doi.org/10.1016/S1364-6613(99)01419-9.

Bartholomew, J. R. (1989). *The formation of science in Japan: Building a research tradition*. Yale University Press.

Bartlett, R. (1986). *Trial by fire and water: The medieval judicial ordeal*. Clarendon Press.

Bascom, W. R. (1941). The sanctions of Ifa divination. *The Journal of the Royal Anthropological Institute of Great Britain and Ireland, 71*(1/2), 43–54.

Beattie, J. (1960). *Bunyoro: An African Kingdom* (pp. ix, 86). Holt. https://ehrafworldcultures.yale.edu/document?id=fk11-002.

Beattie, J., & Middleton, J. (1969). *Spirit mediumship and society in Africa* (J. Beattie & J. Middleton, Eds.). Africana Publishing Corporation.

Bell, L. (2017). Lawfinding, duality and irrationality: Rethinking trial by ordeal in Weber's Economy and Society. *Law and Humanities, 11*(2), 266–285.

Berger, P. L. (1977). Secular theology and the rejection of the supernatural: Reflections on recent trends. *Theological Studies, 38*(1), 39–56.

Berglund, A.-I. (1976). *Zulu thought-patterns and symbolism*. Swedish Institute of missionary research.

Bergstrom, B., Moehlmann, B., & Boyer, P. (2006). Extending the testimony problem: Evaluating the truth, scope, and source of cultural information. *Child Development, 77*(3), 531–538.

Bhawuk, D. P. S. (2010). A perspective on epistemology and ontology of Indian psychology: A synthesis of theory, method and practice. *Psychology and Developing Societies, 22*(1), 157–190.

Blanton, H., Jaccard, J., Christie, C., & Gonzales, P. M. (2007). Plausible assumptions, questionable assumptions and post hoc rationalizations: Will the real IAT, please stand up? *Journal of Experimental Social Psychology, 43*(3), 399–409.

Bloch, M. (2012). *Anthropology and the cognitive challenge*. Cambridge University Press.

Bohannan, P. (1975). Tiv divination. In J. H. M. Beattie & R. G. Lienhardt (Eds.), *Studies in social anthropology* (pp. 149–166). Clarendon.

Bok, B. J., Jerome, L. E., & Kurtz, P. (1975). *Objections to astrology*. Prometheus books.

Booth, N. S. (1978). Tradition and community in African religion. *Journal of Religion in Africa, 9*, 81–94.

Bourdillon, M. F. C. (1976). *The Shona peoples: An ethnography of the contemporary Shona, with special reference to their religion* (Vol. 1). Mambo Press.

Boyd, R., Richerson, P. J., & Henrich, J. (2011). The cultural niche: Why social learning is essential for human adaptation. *Proceedings of the National Academy of Sciences, 108*(supplement_2), 10918–10925.

Boyer, P. (1994). *The naturalness of religious ideas: A cognitive theory of religion*. University of California Press.

Boyer, P. (1996). What makes anthropomorphism natural: Intuitive ontology and cultural representations. *Journal of the Royal Anthropological Institute, 2*, 83–97.

Boyer, P. (2020). Why divination? Evolved psychology and strategic interaction in the production of truth. *Current Anthropology, 61*(1), 100–123. https://doi.org/10.1086/706879.

Bråten, E. (2016). Reading Holbraad: Truth and doubt in the context of ontological inquiry. In B. E. Bertelsen & S. Bendixsen (Eds.), *Critical anthropological engagements in human alterity and difference* (pp. 273–294).

Bremmer, J. (1999). The birth of the term "magic." *Zeitschrift Für Papyrologie Und Epigraphik, 126*, 1–12.

Brown, D. (2006). Astral divination in the context of Mesopotamian divination, medicine, religion, magic, society, and scholarship. *East Asian Science, Technology, and Medicine, 25*(1), 69–126.

Bullivant, S., Farias, M., Lanman, J., & Lee, L. (2019). *Understanding unbelief: Atheists and agnostics around the world.* Technical report St Mary's University, UK. https://www.stmarys.ac.uk/research/centres/benedict-xvi/understanding-unbelief.aspx.

Bunzel, R. L. (1952). *Chichicastenango: A Guatemalan village.* J.J. Augustin.

Burkert, W. (2005). Signs, commands, and knowledge: Ancient divination between enigma and epiphany. In S. I. Johnston & P. T. Struck (Eds.), *Mantikê* (pp. 29–49). Brill.

Burn, A. (1962). *Persia and the Greeks: The defence of the West, c. 546–478 BC.* Edward Arnold.

Cabrera, F. (2020). Evidence and explanation in Cicero's On Divination. *Studies in History and Philosophy of Science Part A, 82*, 34–43.

Caldararo, N. L. (2008). Caching, money, magic, derivatives, mana and modern finance. *Available at SSRN 1007819.*

Carey, S. (1985). *Conceptual change in childhood.* MIT press.

Chalupa, A. (2014). Pythiai and inspired divination in the Delphic Oracle: Can cognitive sciences provide us with an access to "dead minds"? *Journal of Cognitive Historiography, 1*(1), 24–51.

Chen, D. (1915). 今日中国之政治问题. 新青年, *5*(1), 6–9.

Cheng, C.-Y. (2011). The Yijing: The creative origin of Chinese philosophy. In W. Edelglass & J. L. Garfields (Eds.), *The Oxford handbook of world philosophy* (13–25). Oxford Handbooks.

Chuang, R. (2011). Divination/Fortune telling (Zhan Bu/Xianming): Chinese cultural Praxis and Worldview. *China Media Research, 7*(4), 93–103.

Cicero, M. T. (1921). *De divinatione* (Vol. 1). University of Illinois [Press].

Clarke, J. D. (1939). Ifa Divination. *The Journal of the Royal Anthropological Institute of Great Britain and Ireland, 69*(2), 235–256.

Clément, F. (2010). To trust or not to trust? Children's social epistemology. *Review of Philosophy and Psychology, 1*, 531–549.

Cocker, P. J., & Winstanley, C. A. (2015). Irrational beliefs, biases and gambling: Exploring the role of animal models in elucidating vulnerabilities for the development of pathological gambling. *Behavioural Brain Research, 279*, 259–273.

Coggin, P. (2006). Tossing a coin could well be as insightful to investors as a fund manager. *Financial Times, 1*.

Cohen, A. P. (1978). Coercing the rain deities in ancient China. *History of Religions, 17*, 244–265. https://doi.org/10.1086/462793.

Cohen, E. (2007). *The mind possessed: The cognition of spirit possession in an Afro-Brazilian religious tradition*. Oxford University Press.

Colson, E. (1966). The alien diviner and local politics among the Tonga of Zambia. In M. Swartz, V. W. Turner, & A. Tuden (Eds.), *Political anthropology* (pp. 221–228). Aldine Press.

Comaroff, J., & Comaroff, J. L. (2018). Occult economies, revisited. In B. Moeran & T. de Wall Malefyt (Eds.), *Magical capitalism: Enchantment, spells, and occult practices in contemporary economies* (pp. 289–320). Springer.

Cooley, J. L., Pongratz-Leisten, B., Strine, C. A. et al. (2014). *Divination, politics, and ancient near Eastern empires*. Society of Biblical Literature.

Coy, J. (2016). A Christian warning: Bartholomaeus anhorn, demonology, and divination. In K. A. Edwards (Ed.), *Everyday magic in early modern Europe* (pp. 127–146). Routledge.

Cushman, F. (2019). Rationalization is rational. *Behavioral and Brain Sciences, 43*, e28–e28. https://doi.org/10.1017/S0140525X19001730.

D'Andrade, R. G. (1961). Anthropological studies of dreams. In F. L. Hsu (Ed.), *Psychological anthropology: Approaches to culture and personality* (pp. 298–332). Dorsey Press.

David, M. (2022). The correspondence theory of truth. In E. N. Zalta (Ed.), *The Stanford encyclopedia of philosophy* (Summer). Metaphysics Research Lab, Stanford University.

Dawson, L. L. (1999). When prophecy fails and faith persists: A theoretical overview. *Nova Religio, 3*(1), 60–82.

de Barra, M. (2017). Reporting bias inflates the reputation of medical treatments: A comparison of outcomes in clinical trials and online product reviews. *Social Science and Medicine, 177*, 248–255. https://doi.org/10.1016/j.socscimed.2017.01.033.

De Barra, M., Eriksson, K., & Strimling, P. (2014). How feedback biases give ineffective medical treatments a good reputation. *Journal of Medical Internet Research*, *16*, e193. https://doi.org/10.2196/jmir.3214.

Dein, S. (2016). The category of the supernatural: A valid anthropological term? *Religion Compass*, *10*, 35–44. https://doi.org/10.1111/rec3.12194.

Denham, A. R. (2015). A psychodynamic phenomenology of Nankani interpretive divination and the formation of meaning. *Ethos*, *43*(2), 109–134.

Denig, E. T., & Hewitt, J. N. B. (1930). *Indian tribes of the upper Missouri*. Government Printing Office.

Dennett, D. C. (1987). *The intentional stance*. MIT Press.

Denyer, N. (1985). The case against divination: An examination of Cicero's de Divinatione. *The Cambridge Classical Journal*, *31*, 1–10.

Devisch, R. (2013). Perspectives on divination in contemporary sub-Saharan Africa. In W. van Binsbergen & M. Schoffeleers (Eds.), *Theoretical explorations in Africa* (pp. 60–93). Routledge.

Dickson, D. H., & Kelly, I. W. (1985). The "Barnum Effect" in personality assessment: A review of the literature. *Psychological Reports*, *57*(2), 367–382.

Douglas, M. (1975). *Implicit meanings: Essays in anthropology*. Routledge & Kegan Paul.

Driediger-Murphy, L. G. (2019). Unsuccessful sacrifice in Roman state divination. In L. G. Driediger-Murphy & E. Eidinow (Eds.), *Ancient divination and experience* (pp. 178–199). Oxford University Press.

Durkheim, E. (1915). *The Elementary Forms of the Religious Life: A Study in Religious Sociology*. Macmillan.

Eames, K. J. (2016). *Cognitive psychology of religion*. Waveland Press.

Ellis, W. (1917). *A narrative of a tour through Hawaii, or Owhyhee: With remarks on the history, traditions, manners, customs, and language of the inhabitants of the Sandwich Islands* (Issue 2). Hawaiian Gazette.

Elvin, M. (1998). Who was responsible for the weather? Moral meteorology in late imperial China. *Osiris*, *13*, 213–237.

Evans-Pritchard, E. (1937). *Witchcraft, oracles and magic among the Azande*. Clarendon Press.

Faki, E., Kasiera, E. M., & Nandi, O. M. J. (2010). The belief and practice of divination among the Swahili Muslims in Mombasa district, Kenya. *International Journal of Sociology and Anthropology*, *2*(9), 213–223.

Fang, A. (2015). 唐代小说中的占梦文化研究. 新疆师范大学.

Fernandez, J. W. (1967). Divinations, Confessions, Testimonies – Confrontations with the Social Superstructure among Durban Africans. *Occasional Papers of the Institute for Social Research (Winter–Spring) No, 9*.

Ferré, F. (1970). The definition of religion. *Journal of the American Academy of Religion, 38*(1), 3–16.

Festinger, L., Riecken, H., & Schachter, S. (1956). *When prophecy fails*. Harper and Row.

Fiedler, K., & Schwarz, N. (2016). Questionable research practices revisited. *Social Psychological and Personality Science, 7*(1), 45–52.

Figal, G. A. (1999). *Civilization and monsters: Spirits of modernity in Meiji Japan*. Duke University Press.

Fiskesjo, M. (2001). Rising from blood-stained fields: Royal hunting and state formation in Shang China. *Bulletin of the Museum of Far Eastern Antiquities, 73*(49), 48–191.

Flad, R. K. (2008). Divination and power. *Current Anthropology, 49*(3), 403–437. https://doi.org/10.1086/588495.

Flower, M. (2008). *The seer in Ancient Greece*. University of California Press.

Forbes, T. R. (1959). The prediction of sex: Folklore and science. *Proceedings of the American Philosophical Society, 103*(4), 537–544.

Fortes, M. (1966). Religious premises and logical technique in divinatory ritual. *Philosophical Transactions of the Royal Society of London. Series B, Biological Sciences, 251*(772), 409–422.

Foster, K. R., & Kokko, H. (2009). The evolution of superstitious and superstition-like behaviour. *Proceedings of the Royal Society B: Biological Sciences, 276*, 31–37. https://doi.org/10.1098/rspb.2008.0981.

Fourie, P. J. A. (1988). The birth of the mechanistic worldview (and consequently: The redundancy of the God concept). *Scriptura: Journal for Biblical, Theological and Contextual Hermeneutics, 25*, 36–47.

Frankish, K. (2009). Partial belief and flat-out belief. In F. Huber & C. Schmidt-Petri (Eds.), *Degrees of belief* (pp. 75–93). Springer.

Frazer, J. G. (1890). *The golden bough: A study in comparative religion* (Vol. 2). Macmillan.

French, R. (2005). *Ancient natural history: Histories of nature*. Routledge.

Furley, W., & Gysembergh, V. (2015). *Reading the liver: Papyrological texts on ancient Greek extispicy* (Vol. 94). Mohr Siebeck.

Furnham, A., & Schofield, S. (1987). Accepting personality test feedback: A review of the Barnum effect. *Current Psychology, 6*, 162–178.

Gaifman, M. (2018). *The art of libation in classical athens*. Yale University Press.

Geertz, C. (1973). *The interpretation of cultures* (Vol. 5019). Basic books.

Gelfand, M. (1956). *Medicine and magic of the Mashona*. Juta.

Gershman, S. J. (2019). How to never be wrong. *Psychonomic Bulletin and Review, 26*, 13–28. https://doi.org/10.3758/s13423-018-1488-8.

Gigerenzer, G. (2007). *Gut feelings: The intelligence of the unconscious.* Penguin.

Gilbert, D. T., Tafarodi, R. W., & Malone, P. S. (1993). You can't not believe everything you read. *Journal of Personality and Social Psychology, 65*(2), 221–233.

Gmelch, G. (2010). Baseball magic. In P. A. Moro & J. E. Myers (Eds.), *Magic, witchcraft, and religion: A reader in the anthropology of religion* (pp. 320–326). McGrow-Hill.

Goldman, A. I. (1994). Argumentation and social epistemology. *Journal of Philosophy, 91*, 27–49. https://doi.org/10.2307/2940949.

Goody, J. (1961). Religion and ritual: The definitional problem. *The British Journal of Sociology, 12*(2), 142–164.

Greisman, H. C. (1976). "Disenchantment of the world": Romanticism, aesthetics and sociological theory. *The British Journal of Sociology, 27*(4), 495–507.

Griffiths, M. D. (1990). The cognitive psychology of gambling. *Journal of Gambling Studies, 6*(1), 31–42.

Gross, J. (1937). Trial by Ordeal in Ancient Hebrew Law. *Detroit Law Review, 7*, 78–108.

Grout, L. (1864). *Zululand: Or, life among the Zulu-Kafirs of Natal and Zululand, South Africa. With map, and illustrations, largely from original photographs.* Presbyterian.

Gurval, R. A. (1997). Caesar's comet: The politics and poetics of an Augustan myth. *Memoirs of the American Academy in Rome, 42*, 39–71.

Guthrie, S. (1980). A cognitive theory of religion [and comments and reply]. *Current Anthropology, 21*(2), 181–203.

Guthrie, S. (2013). Anthropomorphism. In A. Runehov & L. Oviedo (Eds.), *Encyclopedia of sciences and religions* (pp. 111–113). Springer.

Habkirk, S., & Chang, H. (2017). Scents, community, and incense in traditional Chinese religion. *Material Religion, 13*(2), 156–174.

Hacking, I. (1990). *The taming of chance* (Issue 17). Cambridge University Press.

Hallowell, A. I. [Alfred I.] (1942). The role of conjuring in Saulteaux society. In *Publications* (Vol. 2, pp. xiv, 96). University of Pennsylvania Press [H. Milford, Oxford University Press]. https://ehrafworldcultures.yale.edu/document?id=ng06-004.

Hallowell, A. I. (1960). Ojibwa ontology, behavior, and world view. In S. Diamond (Ed.), *Culture in history: Essays in honor of Paul Radin* (pp. 20–52). Columbia University Press.

Han, X. (2015). 董仲舒天人关系的三维向度及其思想定位. 哲学研究, *9*, 45–54.

Hand, D. J. (2004). *Measurement theory and practice: The world through quantification*. Wiley .

Hanegraaff, W. J. (2003). How magic survived the disenchantment of the world. *Religion*, *33*(4), 357–380.

Hankinson, R. J. (1988). Stoicism, science and divination. *Apeiron*, *21*(2), 123–160.

Harding, S. (1976). *Can theories be refuted? Essays on the Duhem–Quine thesis*. D. Reidel.

Harris, P. (2006). Social cognition. In W. Damon, R. Lerner, D. Kuhn, & R. Siegler (Eds.), *Handbook of child psychology* (6th ed., Vol. 2, pp. 811–858). John Wiley.

Hatsis, T. (2018). *Psychedelic mystery traditions: Spirit plants, magical practices, and ecstatic states*. Simon and Schuster.

Head, M. L., Holman, L., Lanfear, R., Kahn, A. T., & Jennions, M. D. (2015). The extent and consequences of p-hacking in science. *PLoS Biology*, *13*(3), e1002106.

Heald, S. (1991). Divinatory failure: The religious and social role of Gisu diviners. *Africa*, *61*(3), 299–317.

Heindel, M. (2006). *Simplified Scientific Astrology*. Cosimo, Inc.

Heintz, C., & Scott-Phillips, T. (2023). Expression unleashed: The evolutionary and cognitive foundations of human communication. *Behavioral and Brain Sciences*, *46*, e1.

Hempel, C. G. (1966). *Philosophy of natural science*. Prentice-Hall.

Henrich, J. (2009). The evolution of costly displays, cooperation and religion. credibility enhancing displays and their implications for cultural evolution. *Evolution and Human Behavior*, *30*, 244–260. https://doi.org/10.1016/j.evolhumbehav.2009.03.005.

Henrich, J. (2016). *The secret of our success: How culture is driving human evolution, domesticating our species, and making us smarter*. Princeton University Press. https://psycnet.apa.org/record/2016-18797-000.

Henrich, J., & Broesch, J. (2011). On the nature of cultural transmission networks: Evidence from Fijian villages for adaptive learning biases. *Philosophical Transactions of the Royal Society B: Biological Sciences*, *366*(1567), 1139–1148.

Hewitt, J. N. B. (1902). Orenda and a definition of religion. *American Anthropologist*, *4*(1), 33–46.

Hignett, C. (1963). *Xerxes' invasion of Greece*. Clarendon Press.

Hiltunen, M. (1986). Witchcraft and sorcery in Ovambo. In *Transactions of the finnish anthropological society; Suomen Antropologisen Seuran toimituksia* (Issue No. 17, p. 178). Finnish Anthropological Society. https://ehrafworld cultures.yale.edu/document?id=fx08-015.

Hiltunen, M. (1993). *Good magic in Ovambo* (Issue 33). Suomen Antropologinen Seura.

Holbraad, M. (2009). Ontography and alterity: Defining anthropological truth. *Social Analysis, 53*(2), 80–93.

Holbraad, M. (2019). *Truth in motion: The recursive anthropology of Cuban divination.* University of Chicago Press.

Holleman, J. F. (1969). *Shona customary law: With reference to kinship, marriage, the family and the estate.* Manchester University Press.

Homola, S. (2016). Judging destiny: Doubt and certainty in Chinese divinatory rituals. In A. Good, D. Berti, & G. Tarabout (Eds.), *Of doubt and proof* (pp. 39–58). Routledge.

Homola, S. (2019). Reducing uncertainty through computation in Chinese divinatory arts. In D. Schäfer, Z. Lu, & M. Lackner (Eds.), *Accounting for uncertainty: Prediction and planning in Asian history* (pp. 55–68). Preprint 496, Max Planck Institute for the History of Science.

Hones, S., & Endo, Y. (2006). History, distance and text: Narratives of the 1853–1854 Perry expedition to Japan. *Journal of Historical Geography, 32*, 563–578. https://doi.org/10.1016/j.jhg.2005.10.008.

Hong, Z. (2022a). Combining conformist and payoff bias in cultural evolution. *Human Nature, 33*, 463–484.

Hong, Z. (2022b). Dream interpretation from a cognitive and cultural evolutionary perspective: The case of oneiromancy in traditional China. *Cognitive Science, 46*(1), e13088. https://doi.org/10.1111/cogs.13088.

Hong, Z. (2022c). Ghosts, divination, and magic among the Nuosu: An ethnographic examination from cognitive and cultural evolutionary perspectives. *Human Nature, 33*, 349–379. https://doi.org/10.1007/s12110-022-09438-8.

Hong, Z. (2023). The cognitive origin and cultural evolution of taboos in human societies. *Journal of the Royal Anthropological Institute, 30*, 724–742.

Hong, Z. (2024, January 3). Chance as a (non)explanation: A cross-cultural examination of folk understanding of chance and coincidence. PsyArXiv, https://doi.org/10.31234/osf.io/ezxqp.

Hong, Z. (2024). The cultural evolution of games of chance. *Human Nature, 35*, 89–113.

Hong, Z., & Chen, Y. (2024). Persuading the emperors: A quantitative historical analysis of political rhetoric in traditional China. *Humanities and Social Sciences Communications, 11*(1), 1–10.

Hong, Z., & Henrich, J. (2021). The cultural evolution of epistemic practices. *Human Nature, 32*, 622–651.

Hong, Z., & Henrich, J. (2024). Instrumentality, empiricism, and rationality in Nuosu divination. *Religion, Brain & Behavior*, 1–19.

Hong, Z., Slingerland, E., & Henrich, J. (2024). Magic and empiricism in early Chinese rainmaking–A cultural evolutionary analysis. *Current Anthropology, 65*(2), 343–363.

Hong, Z., & Zinin, S. (2023). The psychology and social dynamics of fetal sex prognostication in China: Evidence from historical data. *American Anthropologist, 125*(3), 519–531.

Horton, R. (1960). A definition of religion, and its uses. *The Journal of the Royal Anthropological Institute of Great Britain and Ireland, 90*(2), 201–226.

Horton, R. (1967). African traditional thought and western science. *Africa, 37*, 50–71. https://doi.org/10.2307/1158253.

Horton, R. (1968). Neo-Tylorianism: Sound sense or sinister prejudice? *Man, 3* (4), 625–634. https://doi.org/10.2307/2798583.

Huang, B. (2022). The religious and technological history of the Tang Dynasty spherical incense burner. *Religions, 13*(6), 482.

Hyams, P. (1981). Trial by ordeal: The key to proof in the early common law. In M. S. Arnold, T. A. Green, S. A. Scully, & S. D. White (Eds.), *On the laws and customs of England* (pp. 90–126). University of North Carolina Press.

Jahoda, G. (1970). *The psychology of superstition*, Penguin.

Jarvie, I. C. (1986). *Thinking about society: Theory and practice*. D. Reidel.

Jarvie, I. (2018). Rationality and irrationality revisited or intellectualism vindicated or how stands the problem of the rationality of magic? In G. Bronner & F. Di Iorio (Eds.), *The mystery of rationality: Mind, beliefs and the social sciences* (pp.115–129). Springer.

Jeffers, A. (2007). Interpreting magic and divination in the ancient near east. *Religion Compass, 1*(6), 684–694.

Johnston, S. I. (2001). Charming children: The use of the child in ancient divination. *Arethusa, 34*(1), 97–117.

Johnston, S. I. (2005). Introduction: Divining divination. In S. I. Johnston & P. T. Struck (Eds.), *Mantikê: Studies in ancient divination* (pp. 1–28). Brill.

Johnston, S. I. (2009). Ancient Greek divination. In *Ancient Greek divination*. Wiley. https://doi.org/10.1002/9781444302998.

Jong, J. (2015). On (not) defining (non) religion. *Science, Religion and Culture, 2*(3), 15–24.

Jordan, D. K. (1982). Taiwanese poe divination: Statistical awareness and religious belief. *Journal for the Scientific Study of Religion, 21,* 114–118. https://doi.org/10.2307/1385496.

Jouan, F. (1990). L'orale, thérapeutique de l'angoisse. *Kernos. Revue Internationale et Pluridisciplinaire de Religion Grecque Antique, 3,* 11–28.

Jules-Rosette, B. (1978). The veil of objectivity: Prophecy, divination, and social inquiry. *American Anthropologist, 80*(3), 549–570.

Junod, H. A. (1927). *The life of a South African tribe* (Vol. 2). Macmillan.

Kahneman, D., & Tversky, A. (1972). Subjective probability: A judgment of representativeness. *Cognitive Psychology, 3,* 430–454. https://doi.org/10.1016/0010-0285(72)90016-3.

Kahneman, D., & Tversky, A. (1973). On the psychology of prediction. *Psychological Review, 80*(4), 237–251.

Kamali, E. P. (2018). Trial by ordeal by jury in medieval England, or saints and sinners in literature and law. In K. Gilbert & S. D. White (Eds.), *Emotion, violence, vengeance and law in the Middle Ages* (pp. 49–79). Brill.

Karcher, S. (1998). Divination, synchronicity, and fate. *Journal of Religion and Health, 37*(3), 215–228.

Katz, P. R. (2013). "Superstition" and Its Discontents – on the Impact of Temple Destruction Campaigns in China, 1898–1948. *Belief, Practice and CulturalAdaption* 信仰，實踐與文化調適. *Taipei: Academia Sinica,* 605–682.

Keil, F. C., Levin, D. T., Richman, B. A., & Gutheil, G. (1999). Mechanism and explanation in the development of biological thought: The case of disease. In D. L. Medin & S. Atran (Eds.), *Folkbiology* (pp. 285–319). MIT Press.

Kerridge, I. H., & Lowe, M. (1995). Bloodletting: The story of a therapeutic technique. *The Medical Journal of Australia, 163*(11–12), 631–633. www.ncbi.nlm.nih.gov/pubmed/8538564.

Kiernan, J. P. (1995). The truth revealed or the truth assembled: Reconsidering the role of the African diviner in religion and society. *Journal for the Study of Religion, 8,* 3–21.

Kindt, J. (2006). Delphic oracle stories and the beginning of historiography: Herodotus' Croesus logos. *Classical Philology, 101*(1), 34–51.

Kippenberg, H. G. (1997). Magic in Roman civil discourse: Why rituals could be illegal. In P. Schäfer & H. Kippenberg (Eds.), *Envisioning magic* (pp. 137–163). Brill.

Kitz, A. M. (2003). Prophecy as divination. *The Catholic Biblical Quarterly, 65*(1), 22–42.

Knight, G. R. (1993). *Millennial fever and the end of the world: A study of Millerite Adventism.* Pacific Press.

Kohol, B. N., & Akuto, G. W. (2019). Integration of divination therapy and modern counselling (rational emotive therapy) in combating fear among Tiv undergraduate students in Benue State, Nigeria. *Journal of Culture, Society and Development, 53*, 37–42.

Kuo, C.-L., & Kavanagh, K. H. (1994). Chinese perspectives on culture and mental health. *Issues in Mental Health Nursing, 15*(6), 551–567.

Lai, K. L. (2015). Cosmology, divinity and self-cultivation in Chinese thought. In G. Oppy (Ed.), *The Routledge handbook of contemporary philosophy of religion* (pp. 93–113). Routledge.

Lambert, H. E. (1956). *Kikuyu social and political institutions*. International African Institute.

Landau, M. J., Kay, A. C., & Whitson, J. A. (2015). Compensatory control and the appeal of a structured world. *Psychological Bulletin, 141*(3), 694–722.

Landry, Aa. (2014). *Plato's conception of divination* [Ph.D., York University]. https://yorkspace.library.yorku.ca/xmlui/bitstream/handle/10315/28162/Landry_Aaron_J_2014_PhD.pdf?sequence=2&isAllowed=y.

Landy, J., & Saler, M. (2009). *The Re-enchantment of the World*. Standford University Press.

Langdon, E. J. (2007). The symbolic efficacy of rituals: From ritual to performance. *Antropologia Em Primeira Mão, 95*, 5–40.

Lazaro, C. (2023). Algorithmic divination: From prediction to preemption of the future. *Information & Culture, 58*(2), 145–165.

Leeson, P. T. (2012). Ordeals. *The Journal of Law and Economics, 55*(3), 691–714.

Levy, N. (2022). Do your own research! *Synthese, 200*, 356.

Li, G. (2018). Divination, Yijing, and cultural nationalism: The self-legitimation of divination as an aspect of "traditional culture" in post-Mao China. *China Review, 18*(4), 63–84.

Li, F., & Lang, M. (2012). 近代中国知识转型视野下的 "命学." 社会科学, *6*, 147–154.

Lindeman, M., & Svedholm, A. M. (2012). What's in a term? Paranormal, superstitious, magical and supernatural beliefs by any other name would mean the same. *Review of General Psychology, 16*, 241–255. https://doi.org/10.1037/a0027158.

Lindsay, D. S. (2015). Replication in psychological science. *Psychological Science, 26*(12), 1827–1832. Sage.

Lisdorf, A. (2007). *The dissemination of divination in roman republican times- A cognitive approach*. Anders Lisdorf.

Lock, M. (2005). Eclipse of the gene and the return of divination. *Current Anthropology, 46*(S5), S47–S70.

Lohmann, R. (2003). Special issue: Perspectives on the category "supernatural." *Anthropological Forum, 13*(2), 115–219.

Lupton, D., Donaldson, C., & Lloyd, P. (1991). Caveat emptor or blissful ignorance? Patients and the consumerist ethos. *Social Science & Medicine, 33*(5), 559–568.

Mackey, J. L. (2016). Roman children as religious agents: The cognitive foundations of cult. In C. Laes & V. Vuolanto (Eds.), *Children and everyday life in the Roman and Late Antique world* (pp. 179–197). Routledge.

Ma-Kellams, C. (2015). When perceiving the supernatural changes the natural: Religion and agency detection. *Journal of Cognition and Culture, 15*(3–4), 337–343.

Malinowski, B. (1992). *Magic, science, and religion, and other essays.* Waveland Press. https://books.google.com/books?id=EAESAQAAIAAJ.

Malkowski, E. F. (2007). *The spiritual technology of ancient Egypt: Sacred science and the mystery of consciousness.* Simon and Schuster.

Matthews, W. (2017). Making "science" from "superstition": Conceptions of knowledge legitimacy among contemporary Yijing diviners. *Journal of Chinese Religions, 45*(2), 173–196.

Matthews, W. (2021). Reducing uncertainty: Six lines prediction in contemporary China. In T.-K. Hon (Ed.), *The other Yijing* (pp. 269–301). Brill.

Matthews, W. (2022). Reduction, generation, and truth: A comparative approach to divinatory interpretation. *Current Anthropology, 63*(3), 330–349.

Maxwell, K. B. (1983). *Bemba myth and ritual: The impact of literacy on an oral culture* (Vol. 2). P. Lang.

Maxwell, R. J., & Silverman, P. (1970). Information and esteem: Cultural considerations in the treatment of the aged. *Aging and Human Development, 1*(4), 361–392.

Mbiti, J. S. (1969). *African traditional religions and philosophy.* Heinemann.

McLoughlin, W. G., Conser, W. H., & McLoughlin, V. D. (1984). The Cherokee Ghost Dance movement of 1811–1813. *The Cherokee Ghost Dance: Essays on the Southeastern Indians, 1789–1861*, 111–151.

Mendonsa, E. (1976). Characteristics of Sisala diviners. In A. Bharati (Ed.), *The realm of extra-human agents and audiences* (pp. 179–195). Mouton.

Mercier, H., & Boyer, P. (2021). Truth-making institutions: From divination, ordeals and oaths to judicial torture and rules of evidence. *Evolution and Human Behavior, 42*(3), 259–267.

Metzner, R. (1998). Hallucinogenic drugs and plants in psychotherapy and shamanism. *Journal of Psychoactive Drugs, 30*(4), 333–341.

Miller, D. T., & McFarland, C. (1987). Pluralistic ignorance: When similarity is interpreted as dissimilarity. *Journal of Personality and Social Psychology, 53*(2), 298–305.

Miton, H., Claidière, N., & Mercier, H. (2015). Universal cognitive mechanisms explain the cultural success of bloodletting. *Evolution and Human Behavior, 36*, 303–312. https://doi.org/10.1016/j.evolhumbehav.2015.01.003.

Moss, S. (2018). *Probabilistic knowledge.* Oxford University Press.

Muller, J. (2018). *The tyranny of metrics.* Princeton University Press.

Myhre, K. C. (2006). Divination and experience: Explorations of a Chagga epistemology. *Journal of the Royal Anthropological Institute, 12*(2), 313–330.

Nadel, S. F. (1954). *Nupe religion.* Routledge & Paul. https://ehrafworldcultures.yale.edu/document?id=ff52-002.

Nemeroff, C., & Rozin, P. (2000). The makings of the magical mind: The nature and function of sympathetic magical thinking. In K. S. Rosengren, C. N. Johnson, P. L. Harris, C. N. Johnson, & P. L. Harris (Eds.), *Imagining the impossible* (pp. 1–34). Cambridge University Press. https://doi.org/10.1017/cbo9780511571381.002.

Newman, P. L. (1965). *Knowing the Gururumba.* Holt, Rinehart & Winston.

Nickerson, R. S. (1998). Confirmation bias: A ubiquitous phenomenon in many guises. *Review of General Psychology, 2*, 175–220. https://doi.org/10.1037/1089-2680.2.2.175.

Nordin, A. (2023). Gauging oneiromancy – the cognition of dream content and cultural transmission of (supernatural) divination. *Religion, Brain & Behavior, 14*, 161–182.

Nosek, B. A., Ebersole, C. R., DeHaven, A. C., & Mellor, D. T. (2018). The preregistration revolution. *Proceedings of the National Academy of Sciences of the United States of America. 115*, 2600–2606. https://doi.org/10.1073/pnas.1708274114.

Nürnberger, K. (1975). The Sotho notion of the Supreme Being and the impact of the Christian proclamation. *Journal of Religion in Africa, 7*(Fasc. 3), 174–200.

Obiechina, E. (1975). *Culture, tradition and society in the West African novel.* Cambridge University Press.

Oppenheim, A. L. (1974). A Babylonian diviner's manual. *Journal of Near Eastern Studies, 33*(2), 197–220.

Ostler, S., & Sun, A. (1999). Fetal sex determination: The predictive value of 3 common myths. *Canadian Medical Association Journal, 161*(12), 1525–1526.

Palmié, S. (2007). Genomics, divination, "racecraft." *American Ethnologist, 34*(2), 205–222.

Park, G. K. (1963). Divination and its social contexts. *The Journal of the Royal Anthropological Institute of Great Britain and Ireland, 93*(2), 195–209.

Parsons, R. (1964). *Religion in an African society.* E.J. Brill.

Pasquale, F. L., & Kosmin, B. A. (2013). Atheism and the secularization thesis. In M. Ruse & S. Bullivant (Eds.), *The Oxford handbook of atheism* (pp. 451–467). Oxford University Press.

Peat, F. D. (1994). *Blackfoot physics: A journey into the Native American worldview.* Red Wheel/Weiser.

Pecírková, J. (1985). Divination and politics in the late Assyrian empire. *Archiv Orientalni, 53,* 155–168.

Peek, P. M. (1991). African divination systems: Non-normal modes of cognition. In P. Peek (Ed.), *African divination systems: Ways of knowing* (pp. 193–212). Indiana University Press.

Petrus, T. S., & Bogopa, D. L. (2007). Natural and supernatural: Intersections between the spiritual and natural worlds in African witchcraft and healing with reference to southern Africa. *Indo-Pacific Journal of Phenomenology, 7* (1), 1–10.

Planer, R. J., & Sterelny, K. (2022). The costs of magical thinking and hypervigilance: A comment on Singh 2021. *Current Anthropology, 63*(4), 454–455.

Popper, K. (2005). *The logic of scientific discovery.* Routledge.

Price, R. (1975). *Saramaka social structure: Analysis of a maroon society in Surinam* (Issue 12). Institute of Caribbean Studies, University of Puerto Rico.

Radding, C. M. (1979). Superstition to science: Nature, fortune, and the passing of the medieval ordeal. *The American Historical Review, 84*(4), 945–969.

Radman, Z. (2012). *Knowing without thinking: Mind, action, cognition and the phenomenon of the background.* Springer.

Ramsey, S. D. (2023). Argumentum ex divinatione: Divination and civic argument in the ancient world. *Argumentation, 37*(3), 419–436.

Raphals, L. A. (2013). *Divination and prediction in early China and ancient Greece.* Cambridge University Press.

Rapisarda, S. (2022). Analogy at work in western medieval divination. In K. Herbers & H.-C. Lehner (Eds.), *Dreams, nature, and practices as signs of the future in the middle ages* (pp. 175–189). Brill.

Reiner, E. (1995). *Astral magic in Babylonia.* American Philosophical Society.

Richardson, S. F. C. (2010). On seeing and believing: Liver divination and the era of warring states (II). In A. Annus (Ed.), *Divination and interpretation of signs in the ancient world* (pp. 225–266). Oriental Institute of the University of Chicago.

Richerson, P. J., & Boyd, R. (2005). *Not by genes alone: How culture transformed human evolution.* University of Chicago Press.

Ringma, C., & Brown, C. (1991). Hermeneutics and the social sciences: An evaluation of the function of hermeneutics in a consumer disability study. *Journal of Sociology and Social Welfare, 18*, 57.

Robertson, R. (2018). Divination. *Psychological Perspectives, 61*(2), 170–193.

Rochberg, F. (2004). *The heavenly writing: Divination, horoscopy, and astronomy in Mesopotamian culture.* Cambridge University Press.

Rohr, C. (2022). Between astrological divination, local knowledge and political intentions: Prognostics and "epignostics" related to natural disasters in the Middle Ages. In K. Herbers & H.-C. Lehner (Eds.), *Dreams, nature, and practices as signs of the future in the middle ages* (pp. 128–172). Brill.

Rozin, P., & Nemeroff, C. (1990). The laws of sympathetic magic: A psychological analysis of similarity and contagion. In J. W. Stigler, R. A. Shweder, & G. H. Herdt (Eds.), *Cultural psychology: Essays on comparative human development* (pp. 205–232). Cambridge University Press.

Rozin, P., & Nemeroff, C. (2012a). Sympathetic magical thinking: The contagion and similarity "heuristics." In T. Gilovich, D. Griffin, & D. Kahneman (Eds.), *Heuristics and biases* (pp. 201–216). Cambridge University Press. https://doi.org/10.1017/cbo9780511808098.013.

Rozin, P., & Nemeroff, C. (2012b). The laws of sympathetic magic. In J. W. Stigler, R. A. Shweder, & G. Herdt (Eds.), *Cultural psychology: Essays on comparative human development* (pp. 205–232). Cambridge University Press. https://doi.org/10.1017/cbo9781139173728.006.

Sahlins, M. (2022). *The new science of the enchanted universe: An anthropology of most of humanity.* Princeton University Press.

Saler, B. (1977). Supernatural as a western category. *Ethos, 5*(1), 31–53.

Saniotis, A. (2007). Mystical mastery: The presentation of Kashf in Sufi divination. *Asian Anthropology, 6*(1), 29–51.

Sawden, K. (2018). This I know to be true: Ethnology, divination and the processes of authenticity. *Ethnologies, 40*(2), 93–110.

Scott, M. (2014). *Delphi: A history of the center of the ancient world.* Princeton University Press.

Semetsky, I. (2011). Tarot and a new science. In I. Semetsky (Ed.), *Re-symbolization of the self* (pp. 157–168). Brill.

Sharples, R. W. (1983). *Alexander of Aphrodisias on Fate.* Duckworth.

Shipley, B. (2016). *Cause and correlation in biology: A user's guide to path analysis, structural equations and causal inference with R.* Cambridge university press.

Silva, S. (2014). Mind, body and spirit in basket divination: An integrative way of knowing. *Religions, 5*(4), 1175–1187.

Silva, S. (2018). Taking divination seriously: From mumbo jumbo to world-views and ways of life. *Religions*, *9*(12), 394.

Simmons, L. W. (1945). *The role of the aged in primitive society.* Yale University Press.

Singh, M. (2022). Subjective selection and the evolution of complex culture. *Evolutionary Anthropology: Issues, News, and Reviews*, *31*(6), 266–280.

Skowronski, J. J., & Carlston, D. E. (1987). Social judgment and social memory: The role of cue diagnosticity in negativity, positivity, and extremity biases. *Journal of Personality and Social Psychology*, *52*(4), 689–699. https://doi.org/10.1037/0022-3514.52.4.689.

Skowronski, J. J., & Carlston, D. E. (1989). Negativity and extremity biases in impression formation: A review of explanations. *Psychological Bulletin*, *105*(1), 131–142. https://doi.org/10.1037//0033-2909.105.1.131.

Smart, W. M. (1946). John Couch Adams and the discovery of Neptune. *Nature*, *158*(4019), 648–652.

Smith, R. J. (1986). "Knowing Fate": Divination in Late Imperial China. *Journal of Chinese Studies*, *3*(2), 153–190.

Smith, R. J. (2010). The Psychology of Divination in Cross-Cultural Perspective. In *Conference Ming and Fatum–key concepts of fate and prediction in a comparative perspective, International Consortium for Research in the Humanities, University of Erlangen-Nürnberg* (Vol. 1, p. 21).

Snoek, J. A. M. (2006). Defining "rituals." In J. Kreinath, J. A. M. Snoek, & M. Stausberg (Eds.), *Theorizing rituals, Volume 1: Issues, topics, approaches, concepts* (pp. 1–14). Brill.

Sørensen, J. (2007). *A cognitive theory of magic.* Rowman Altamira.

Sørensen, J. F. (2021). Cognitive underpinnings of divinatory practices. In J. F. Sørensen & A. K. Petersen (Eds.), *Theoretical and empirical investigations of divination and magic* (pp. 124–150). Brill.

Sørensen, J. F., & Petersen, A. K. (2021). Manipulating the divine–an introduction. In J. F. Sørensen & A. K. Petersen (Eds.), *Theoretical and empirical investigations of divination and magic* (pp. 1–20). Brill.

Soroka, S., Fournier, P., & Nir, L. (2019). Cross-national evidence of a negativity bias in psychophysiological reactions to news. *Proceedings of the National Academy of Sciences of the United States of America*, *116*(38), 18888–18892. https://doi.org/10.1073/pnas.1908369116.

Sperber, D., Clément, F., Heintz, C. et al. (2010). Epistemic vigilance. *Mind and Language*, *25*(4), 359–393. https://doi.org/10.1111/j.1468-0017.2010.01394.x.

Stahlberg, D., & Maass, A. (1997). Hindsight bias: Impaired memory or biased reconstruction? *European Review of Social Psychology*, *8*(1), 105–132. https://doi.org/10.1080/14792779643000092.

Stark, R. (1996). Why religious movements succeed or fail: A revised general model. *Journal of Contemporary Religion, 11*(2), 133–146.

Stépanoff, C. (2015). Transsingularities: The cognitive foundations of shamanism in Northern Asia. *Social Anthropology/Anthropologie Sociale, 23*(2), 169–185.

Stocking Jr., G. W. (1986). Anthropology and the science of the irrational. *Malinowski, Rivers, Benedict and Others: Essays on Culture and Personality, 4,* 23–49.

Struck, P. T. (2016). *Divination and human nature: A cognitive history of intuition in classical antiquity.* Princeton University Press.

Subbotsky, E. (2010). *Magic and the mind: Mechanisms, functions, and development of magical thinking and behavior.* Oxford University Press.

Summers, J. S. (2017). Post hoc ergo propter hoc: Some benefits of rationalization. *Philosophical Explorations, 20*(sup1), 21–36.

Sun, X., & Kistemaker, J. (1997). *The Chinese sky during the Han: Constellating stars and society* (Vol. 38). Brill.

Swedberg, R. (2020). On the use of definitions in sociology. *European Journal of Social Theory, 23*(3), 431–445.

Swerdlow, N. M. (1999). *Ancient astronomy and celestial divination.* MIT Press.

Tedlock, B. (2001). Divination as a way of knowing: Embodiment, visualisation, narrative, and interpretation. *Folklore, 112*(2), 189–197.

Tempels, P. (1945). *La Philosophie Bantoue.* Lovania.

Theuws, T. (1964). Outline of Luba culture. *Cashiers of Economiques et Sociaux, 2*(1), 3–39.

Thomas, K. (2003). *Religion and the decline of magic: Studies in popular beliefs in sixteenth and seventeenth-century England.* Penguin.

Tseng, L. L. (2011). *Picturing heaven in early China.* Harvard University Press.

Turnbull, C. M. (1965). *Wayward servants: The two worlds of the African Pygmies.* The Natural History Press. https://ehrafworldcultures.yale.edu/document?id=fo04-002.

Turner, V. W. (1968). *The drums of affliction: A study of religious processes among the Ndembu of Zambia.* Clarendon Press.

Turner, V. (1975). *Revelation and divination in Ndembu ritual.* Cornell University Press.

Tversky, A., & Kahneman, D. (1973). Availability: A heuristic for judging frequency and probability. *Cognitive Psychology, 5,* 207–232. https://doi.org/10.1016/0010-0285(73)90033-9.

Tversky, A., & Kahneman, D. (1974). Judgment under uncertainty: Heuristics and biases: Biases in judgments reveal some heuristics of thinking under uncertainty. *Science, 185*(4157), 1124–1131.

Tylor, E. B. (1871). *Primitive culture: Researches into the development of mythology, philosophy, religion, art, and custom.* J. Murray.

van Beek, W. E. A. (2015). Evil and the art of revenge in the Mandara mountains. In W. C. Olsen & W. E. A. van Beek (Eds.), *Evil in Africa: Encounters with the everyday* (pp. 140–156). Indiana University Press.

Van Beek, W. E. A., Blakely, T., & Thomson, D. L. (1994). The innocent sorcerer; coping with evil in two African societies, Kapsiki and Dogon. *African Religion: Experience and Expression, 4,* 196–228.

Van Binsbergen, W., & Wiggermann, F. (2000). Magic in history: A theoretical perspective, and its application to Ancient Mesopotamia. In T. Abusch, & K. Van der Toorn (Eds.), *Mesopotamian magic: Textual, historical and interpretative perspectives* (pp. 3–34). Brill.

Van Leeuwen, N. (2014). Religious credence is not factual belief. *Cognition, 133*(3), 698–715.

Van Nuffelen, P. (2014). Galen, divination and the status of medicine1. *The Classical Quarterly, 64*(1), 337–352.

Vance, B. E. (2017). Deciphering dreams: How glyphomancy worked in late Ming dream encyclopedic divination. *The Chinese Historical Review, 24*(1), 5–20.

Vernon, J. L. (2017). Understanding the butterfly effect. *American Scientist, 105*(3), 130.

Voas, D., & Chaves, M. (2016). Is the United States a counterexample to the secularization thesis? *American Journal of Sociology, 121*(5), 1517–1556.

Vyse, S. A. (1997). *Believing in magic: The psychology of superstition.* Oxford University Press.

Waley, A. (1958). *The opium war through Chinese eyes.* Stanford University Press. https://doi.org/10.1515/9781503620711.

Walsham, A. (2008). Recording superstition in early modern Britain: The origins of folklore. *Past and Present, 199*(suppl_3), 178–206.

Wang, Q. E. (1999). History, space, and ethnicity: The Chinese worldview. *Journal of World History, 10,* 285–305.

Wax, M., & Wax, R. (1963). The notion of magic. *Current Anthropology, 4*(5), 495–518.

Waytz, A., Gray, K., Epley, N., & Wegner, D. M. (2010a). Causes and consequences of mind perception. *Trends in Cognitive Sciences, 14*(8), 383–388.

Waytz, A., Morewedge, C. K., Epley, N. et al. (2010b). Making sense by making sentient: Effectance motivation increases anthropomorphism. *Journal of Personality and Social Psychology, 99*(3), 410–435.

Weber, M. (1922). *The sociology of religion*. Methuen.

Wester, J., Delaunay, J., de Jong, S., & van Berkel, N. (2023). On Moral Manifestations in Large Language Models. *Proc. CHI Workshop on Moral Agents*, 1–4.

Willard, A. K., Turpin, H., & Baimel, A. (2023). Universal cognitive biases as the basis for supernatural beliefs: Evidence and critiques. In J. J. Tehrani, J. Kendal, & R. Kendal (Eds.), *The Oxford handbook of cultural evolution*. Oxford University Press.

Wilson, M. H. (1959). *Communal rituals of the Nyakyusa*. Oxford University Press.

Wilson, D., & Sperber, D. (2012). *Meaning and relevance*. Cambridge University Press.

Winzeler, R. L. (2012). *Anthropology and religion: What we know, think, and question*. Rowman & Littlefield.

Wootton, D. (2007). *Bad medicine: Doctors doing harm since Hippocrates*. Oxford University Press.

Xiong, Y. (2015). 近代中国读书人的命理世界. 学术月刊, *47*(9), 147–160.

Yogeeswaran, K., Złotowski, J., Livingstone, M. et al. (2016). The interactive effects of robot anthropomorphism and robot ability on perceived threat and support for robotics research. *Journal of Human-Robot Interaction, 5*(2), 29–47.

Yu, C. K.-C. (2022). Imperial dreams and oneiromancy in ancient China – we share similar dream motifs with our ancestors living two millennia ago. *Dreaming, 32*(4), 364–373.

Zeitlyn, D. (2012). Divinatory logics: Diagnoses and predictions mediating outcomes. *Current Anthropology, 53*(5), 525–546.

Zeitlyn, D. (2021). Divination and ontologies: A reflection. *Social Analysis, 65*(2), 139–160.

Zempléni, A. (1975). De la persécution à la culpabilité. *Prophétisme et Thérapeutique, Paris, Hermann*, 153–219.

Zhang, D. (2002). *Key concepts in Chinese philosophy* (E. Ryden, Ed.). Yale University Press.

Zhang, J., & Huang, Y. (1990). 中國古代天文對政治的影響— 以漢相翟方進自殺為例. 清華學報, *20*(2), 361–378.

Zhiwei, X. (2009). A discourse construction and the institution practice of "Otherization" – a rethinking of anti-superstition movement from Late Qing to Republic of China. *Academic Monthly, 7*, 130–141.

Zhu, A. (2013). 民国时期的反迷信运动与民间信仰空间 – – 以粤西地区为例. 文化遗产, *2*, 112–120.

Zhu, X. (1987). *Zhouyi Benyi* 周易本義. Shanghai Guji Chubanshe.

Zuesse, E. M. (1975). Divination and deity in African religions. *History of Religions*, *15*(2), 158–182.

Acknowledgments

I am grateful to Dr. Aiyana Willard for introducing me to the opportunity to write this Element. I also extend my sincere thanks to Dr. Pascal Boyer, the series editor Dr. Jonathan Lewis-Jong, and two anonymous reviewers for their valuable and constructive feedback on earlier versions of the manuscript.

For EU product safety concerns, contact us at Calle de José Abascal, 56–1°,
28003 Madrid, Spain or eugpsr@cambridge.org.